"I read many books, but seldom do I enjoy one more than I did Tony Reinke's *Lit!* Many of my greatest childhood adventures, and much of my growth after I was converted as a teenager, came through reading imagination-expanding and life-changing books. Tony's writing is thoughtful, perceptive, concise, and God-honoring. He upholds biblical authority and offers helpful guidance, while allowing for a range of tastes. *Lit!* rings true to my own lifetime of reading experience. As a reader and writer of both nonfiction and fiction, I appreciate the breadth of Tony's treatment, which includes a variety of genres. For book lovers, this is a treasure and delight. For those who aren't book lovers, it makes a great case for becoming one."

Randy Alcorn, founder, Eternal Perspective Ministries;
author, *If God Is Good* and *Heaven*

"If you don't read books as both a discipline and a delight, then you should; and if you need help here, as in truth all of us do, then this is the book for you. Don't miss it!"

J. I. Packer, Board of Governors' Professor of Theology, Regent College;
author, *Knowing God*

"This is the perfect book for someone who doesn't like to read, or who likes to read but isn't sure it's a good use of their time, or who loves to read a little too much and needs to proceed with discernment. Reinke has made a wise, theological, and edifying case for why words matter. I'll mention *Lit!* every time someone asks me why in the world Christians should read fiction—a question that never fails to shock me. Now, instead of snapping, 'Are you serious?' and spouting opinions, I'll just smile and slip them a copy of this book."

Andrew Peterson, singer/songwriter;
author, *On the Edge of the Dark Sea of Darkness*

"There is so much to commend about this book that it is hard to know where to start. The most obvious virtue is its scope. On the subject of reading, Reinke covers every possible topic. Each topic, in turn, is broken into all of its important subpoints. With a lesser writer, this could produce a tedious book, but the opposite is true here. Reinke says just enough, but not too much. The effect is like seeing a prism turned in the light. There is never a dull moment. Once I sensed that Reinke was going to cover all the important topics, and with unfailing good sense and Christian insight, I could hardly put it down. 'What will Reinke say about *that* topic?' I found myself asking. But to add yet another twist, he has read so widely in scholarly and religious sources that I do not hesitate to call the book a triumph of scholarship. Reinke writes with an infectious and winsome enthusiasm. It is hard to imagine a reader of this book who would not catch the spark for reading after encountering Reinke's excitement about reading and his carefully reasoned defense of it."

Leland ᴾ⁻ ⁱ ⁱ   ᵃ ᵉssor of English, Wheaton, College;
  ᵗᵉ *ESV and the English Bible Legacy*

"How to read ... and why you should read—Tony Reinke answ ... ry good and (surprisingly) brief book on readi ... to God and growth to the church, Reinke encou ... .c of reading widely and wisely."

Trevin Wax, editor, LifeWay Christian Resources;
author, *Holy Subversion: Allegiance to Christ in an Age of Rivals*

"Since God decided ideas are best expressed in words, and that The Idea—the revelation of his Son as Lord and Savior—is to be learned through his timeless and matchless Word, Christians dare not lose sight of the primacy of books amidst the torrent of fast-moving, visual images of our culture. Tony Reinke argues from Scripture and life experience that 'reading is a way to preserve and cultivate the sustained linear concentration we need for life.' As an educator, I couldn't agree more! Sustained reading must remain the heartbeat of any worthy educational program that seeks to produce Christian thinkers, leaders, and apologists. Homeschooling parents who are trying to craft reading lists as they raise Christian children will find gracious and principled guidance here. Moreover, Tony offers great ideas for parents to foster a love for reading, beginning with their own example."

Marcia Somerville, president, Lampstand Press;
author, the Tapestry of Grace homeschool curriculum

"You might wonder why you need to read about reading. Some of you have piles and piles of books on your shelves, or on your nightstand, but have no idea how to choose what to read, and when. Some of you are being altered in ways you don't even recognize by digital technology such that you can't see how you're too distracted to summon the deep attention needed to read. This engagingly written book will make you think, but it will also provide practical, winsome advice on how to become the right kind of reader for the glory of God."

Russell D. Moore, Dean, Southern Baptist Theological Seminary;
author, *Tempted and Tried*

"Tony Reinke does not just read, but he reads well, and these are two very different things. If you are not much of a reader, consider *Lit!* a part of your education. Tony will teach you to read, to read widely, and to read well. If you are already an avid reader, consider *Lit!* an investment that will instruct you in how to read better."

Tim Challies, blogger, www.challies.com;
author, *The Discipline of Spiritual Discernment*

"If you read one book a week for the next 50 years, you'll read about 2,600 books. Not a lot when you think of all the books you *could* read. So should you include this book in your list? Yes! Because *Lit!* will help you read the right books in the right way. Tony Reinke sets our reading in a biblical framework and provides practical tips to make the most of books. I warmly commend it."

Tim Chester, Director, The Porterbrook Institute;
author, *You Can Change* and *A Meal with Jesus*

"With a discerning eye, Reinke captures the importance of the gospel story for our habits of reading, thus providing a worldview for reading. He challenges us to beware of how the carved images of the Internet can draw us away from the grace of reading for comprehension and simple delight. Yet he equally gives a proper place to secular literature among all types of works that those who love Christ should appreciate. This is the sort of book that I have longed to place into the hands of believers in order to help churches recapture a love for literature and literacy—both biblical and extrabiblical. Practical and enjoyable, *Lit!* is an outstanding and valuable gift to the church."

Eric C. Redmond, Senior Pastor, Reformation Alive Baptist Church,
Temple Hills, Maryland

Lit!

Lit!

A CHRISTIAN GUIDE TO READING BOOKS

TONY REINKE

WHEATON, ILLINOIS

Interior design and typesetting: Lakeside Design Plus
Cover image and design: Jon McGrath, Simplicated Studio
Interior illustration: Painting on page 50: Weyden, Rogier (Roger) van der (c.1399-1464), *The Damned Plunging into Hell*. Detail of the Last Judgment, 1434; Photo credit: Erich Lessing / Art Resource, NY

First printing 2011
Printed in the United States of America

Trade Paperback ISBN: 978-1-4335-2226-0
PDF ISBN: 978-1-4335-2227-7
Mobipocket ISBN: 978-1-4335-2228-4
ePub ISBN: 978-1-4335-2229-1

Library of Congress Cataloging-in-Publication Data
Reinke, Tony, 1977–
    Lit! : a Christian guide to reading books / Tony Reinke ; foreword by C. J. Mahaney.
        p. cm.
    Includes bibliographical references and index.
    ISBN 978-1-4335-2226-0 (trade pbk.)
      1. Christians—Books and reading. 2. Reading. I. Title.
Z1039.C47R45 2011
028'.8—dc23

                                    2011020713

Crossway is a publishing ministry of Good News Publishers.

VP   22   21   20   19   18   17   16   15   14   13   12   11
14   13   12   11   10   9   8   7   6   5   4   3   2   1

Contents

Contents

"In your light do we see light."
Psalm 36:9

Foreword

C. J. Mahaney

Growing up, I hated to read.

Except for two things: as a teenager, I read *The Washington Post* sports page and *Sports Illustrated*. After the *Post* arrived on our doorstep each morning, my dad read the sports page, then my older brother, then me. (And if I ever got hold of it before my brother did, the consequences could be severe.) *Sports Illustrated* got devoured weekly as soon as it arrived.

But aside from those two things, I simply did not read. I did not read any other part of the newspaper. I did not read the books I was assigned in high school (and I have the grades to prove it). I didn't even read CliffsNotes thoroughly—they were too long! I had one passion: sports. I put my school books in my locker, where I thought they belonged. Reading had no place in my life.

By the time I graduated from high school, I'd picked up a few more passions: partying, drinking, and drugs. I was, sadly, immersed in the drug culture, pursuing pleasure as passionately as I could, and recruiting others to join me. I had absolutely no use for books of any kind, least of all the Bible.

So I thought nothing of it when my friend Bob, with whom I had partied frequently before he moved away, called to say he was coming to visit. I was unaware that Bob had been converted, and that his visit would mark a turning point in my life.

Bob came in and like always, I prepared my room for another drug fest, putting a rolled-up towel at the base of the bedroom door so my family supposedly couldn't smell the smoke. (It never worked.) I offered Bob some hash, was momentarily perplexed when he declined, and began to smoke anyway. Then Bob began to share the gospel with me.

That night the impossible happened: in that smoke-filled room, God in his sovereign mercy acted upon my heart, and I experienced the miracle of regeneration. I believed, I turned from my rebellion, and I trusted in the Savior for the forgiveness of my countless sins. The worst of sinners, in the midst of his sin, was born again.

I don't remember every detail of that evening, but I do know that Bob eventually left, and I began reading a King James Bible that he must have left behind. I stayed up all night reading it. I was even underlining it. I didn't understand much of what I read, but I was beginning to perceive eternal life revealed in those words. I was seeing a relationship between the gospel I'd heard, the new birth I'd just received, and this book. And I had an insatiable hunger to read it.

So if you had met me the next day and asked me for evidences of my conversion, high on my list would have been this new, miraculous appetite for reading. And if you had known me, you would have been shocked: the guy who never read books, who was immersed in the drug culture, who was passionate about partying—now this guy could not get enough of a King James Bible.

In spite of all my theological ignorance (which was massive), I knew that Christ loved me and gave himself for me on the cross. And I knew there was life in his words.

Not long after that I got a job at a Christian bookstore just so I could read as much as possible. Boxes of books would arrive daily. Every day was like Christmas! I would assemble stacks of books on the counter and start reading, assuming this was my role: to read the books. And in my immaturity, I viewed customers as an interruption to my reading. I shouldn't have been surprised when my manager eventually informed me that I wasn't hired to read; I was actually supposed to put the books on the shelves. That took some of the joy out of the job.

In the years that followed, various kind and wise people—no doubt seeing my uninformed zeal and desperate need for instruction—began to give me books. The formal education I wanted (another evidence of conversion!) never became possible. But reading—primarily Scripture, and then other books, many of them given to me by these friends—made all the difference in my life and ministry.

Books by authors like Charles Spurgeon, D. A. Carson, R. C. Sproul, Sinclair Ferguson, David Powlison, J. C. Ryle, Jerry Bridges, John Owen, J .I. Packer, John Stott, Wayne Grudem, and so many more—these books helped me understand Holy Scripture. They preached the gospel to me. They taught me to think deeply about the gospel and to preach the gospel to my own soul. This is vital, because thinking deeply about the gospel is the only way to consistently feel deeply about the gospel. You cannot cultivate affection for the Savior without reading and studying the Word of God.

I am even more grateful for these books when I imagine what the last forty years of my life would have been like without them. I would have been vulnerable to every wind of doctrine. I would have assigned ultimate authority to my own emotions or possibly to some personal experience. I would not have grown in my understanding of the gospel. Apart from the mercy of God, I would have continued to read nothing but the *Post* sports page and *Sports Illustrated*, and eventually shipwrecked my faith. (And I'd probably be calling in to sports talk shows daily, arguing obnoxiously about the latest stupid free agent signing by the Redskins, as if sports were all that mattered.)

That's why I'm so excited that my friend Tony has written the book you hold in your hands. Though I now love to read, it's still work. It always involves discipline. Perhaps reading is a challenge for you. Maybe you despised reading in college, and one of the joys of your graduation was the thought that you would never have to read a book again! Then your pastor or other Christians started recommending books. Now you look at the books on your shelves and see a few that you've started, but not one that you've finished. Perhaps you haven't read through the whole Bible yet, but you would never divulge that information to anyone. If that's you, here's what you need to know: *Lit!* is a book for nonreaders.

So let me prepare you for what you'll find in this book. Tony is not like your college profs, burying you under reading assignments in books that should only be used as doorstops. Instead, Tony will give you hope that reading can make a difference in your life. He'll kindle your appetite for reading. He'll provide you with expectations that are realistic and practices that are achievable. You won't be discouraged; instead you'll be hopeful—and you'll actually want to read. And most of all, you'll find that Tony leads you to keep the cross of Christ central in all the reading you do.

I wish I had received a copy of this book when I was just converted. It would have focused my youthful zeal and taught me what to read and how to read it. But you have a copy of it now. And I'm grateful you do. Because I think you will be surprised by the difference it makes in your life.

Introduction

Perhaps you love to read. You get the same feeling from a new stack of books as you get from looking at a warm stack of glazed donuts. Maybe not. For most, reading a book is like trying to drink down a huge vitamin. You know you need to read—you'll be healthier for it—but everything within you refuses to swallow!

Reading books is hard work. A world of reading distractions doesn't make it any easier. Our email inboxes *ding* with new messages, our phones *beep* with new texts, and the Internet lures us with new blog posts and video clips. Meanwhile, streams of social media in our life (like Facebook and Twitter) fill our screens constantly. Dare to look away, and you'll miss the conversation!

Yet here you are reading a book, unplugged and disconnected. Or maybe you are reading with a book in one hand and a smartphone in the other. Like the pull of gravity keeping us in our seats, our attraction to those illuminated screens can become so habitual that we never really think about it. The screens intrude, the free time we need to read books gets sucked away, and our attention gets divided.

Maybe you don't read because you think sitting in one spot for more than fifteen minutes is a waste of time. You've got to be "doing something," and reading feels like "doing nothing."

Or perhaps you don't read because when you're not working or sleeping or going to school you'd rather veg in front of television sitcoms, watch ESPN, and game the night away.

We all have our own reasons for why we don't read.

Lit! A Christian Guide to Reading Books is for any Christian who wants to read books, and read them well. This book covers a wide range of topics: why we should read books in the first place, how to choose the best books, how to find time to read books, and how to find joy—not drudgery—in the pages of books.

This book is particularly relevant to Christians, to men and women who have discovered the deep reality of their own sin and who now trust in the work of Jesus Christ for the forgiveness of those sins. The work of God's grace in your life is the solid foundation that supports lifelong reading goals.

Lit!

This book is all about light, but not the flickering illumination of a computer screen, smartphone, or television. The short title—*Lit!*—represents three things.

First, *lit* is short for *literature*, which is long for *books,* which is the topic of this book. *Lit* is a tiny word that represents many millions of books we can pick up and read.

Second, *lit* reminds us that the glow of God's creative power is all around us. God is the Supreme Being in the universe—supremely true, supremely good, supremely beautiful. He is an extravagant Creator, and his truth, goodness, and beauty are soaked deeply into his creation. In fact, "the whole earth is full of his glory!" (Isa. 6:3). Even in its fallen condition, creation continues to emit the Creator's glory, a glow that can be found in the pages of great books.[1] In this sense, so much "mere human" writing is truly *lit* by God, glowing as a result of his creating power and shining to the praise of his glory.

Third, and most importantly, *lit* represents a conviction underlying this entire book: Christian readers are illuminated by "the light of the gospel of the glory of Christ" (2 Cor. 4:4). "In him was life, and the life was the light of men" (John 1:4). Illuminated by the gospel, we now perceive and enjoy God's truth, goodness, and beauty—whether it's in the blazing sun of the inspired Word of God, in the moonlight of creation, or in the starlight of great books. The Holy Spirit has opened our spiritual eyes, and our entire reading experience is now "lit" by God's illuminating presence.

As strange as it sounds, our eyes are filled with the Creator's glory in literature because we read in the presence of God's radiance. The motto of the reading Christian is a dazzling doxology: "in your light do we see light" (Ps. 36:9).[2] Christian readers can now see and treasure the truth, goodness, and beauty that flicker in the pages of books. The whole thing is like reading books under high voltage stadium lights. We see by the illuminating grace of God.

Quest by Questions

For all that it does do for us, however, divine illumination does not make book reading easy. In fact reading will always present us with several challenges. Before I wrote this book, I listed common questions that surfaced in my own reading, such as:

- What makes reading books like swallowing a large vitamin?
- Why should I prioritize book reading in the first place?
- What do I lose if I don't read books?
- What biblical convictions must I have before I shop at the bookstore?
- Does the gospel really shape *how* I read books? How so?
- What books should I read?
- What books should I *not* read?
- Should I read non-Christian books? Why or why not?
- How can I best read nonfiction books?
- What, if anything, can a Christian gain from reading fictional literature?
- How can I determine the difference between good fiction and bad fiction?
- Where do I find all the time I need to read books?
- Should I write marginal notes in my books?
- What are the pros and cons of reading books on an e-reader device?
- How can I encourage my friends to read books?

- How can I use books and reading groups to encourage other Christians and to build my local church?

Those questions launched me on a quest for answers. In this book I address each question as directly as possible—thanks to Scripture, a few teachers in church history, some old books, a few new books, my friends, and my own experience (mostly mistakes).

This book separates into two main sections: (1) a theology of reading books and (2) a collection of practical suggestions for reading books.

Short, Sweet

This book is short and to the point, or at least as short as I could possibly make it. The shortest chapters are short because they could be short; the longer chapters are longer because there was no possible way to make them shorter.

This commitment to brevity also means I make points quickly and briefly. The danger of brevity is that my suggestions may sound to some readers like edicts. Please remember whenever I give advice in this book, it is nothing more than that—advice. It's not a law or a command. Please listen to the advice, try it out, learn from it, improve it, or simply drop kick what doesn't work for you.

My prayer is that under his illuminating grace, God will be glorified as we read books full of his truth to be discovered, his goodness to be heeded, and his beauty to be cherished.

PART I

A Theology of Books and Reading

I

Paper Pulp and Etched Granite

Laying the Cornerstone of Our Theology of Books

Commit yourself to the serious reading of books, and your life will be enlightened.

That's a pretty straightforward promise, but let's be honest, there is a warning as well: books will also complicate your life.

Consider the complexities we face by walking through a bookstore. Here's how it typically works for me.

First, I start out excited. I've been looking forward to this trip to the bookstore because I need a great book. Before I even swing open the doors, I'm greeted by clearance books—hundreds of them—daring me to look at their discounted tags. What should I do? Should I give attention to these unsheltered books that got kicked to the curb? I'm suspicious. I do my best to ignore them, and suddenly feel the urge to whistle, look to the sky, and comment on the weather.

Once I'm inside the bookstore, a greater challenge awaits: the new releases. These books draw the most attention from shoppers and apparently draw the most money from their wallets (full retail price). But the browsing is good, and there are a lot of attractive book choices.

After picking up a few books (then setting them down again), I free myself from the new releases and convince myself that an older (and more proven) book would be a better investment. So I snake my way through the maze of head-down statues and find open spaces in the Christian book section. Very few of these titles are new to me. I pick up one or two and flip through the pages.

Before long, my curiosity draws me to the rural reaches of classic literature on shelves that reach to the heavens (do shoppers buy many books that are shelved nine feet off the floor?). Here in classic literature, the crowds have thinned, but the browsing is more daunting and incriminating. Many of these books are classics that I should have *already* read. I am shamed for my inattention in school.

My hanging head notices an eight-hundred–page Russian novel by Fyodor Dostoyevsky. The book cover is beautifully designed, the book was translated into English with great care (according to a friend of mine), and the novel is reasonably priced. My eye has caught the spine of this book many times before, and I've nearly purchased it on several of my frequent trips to the bookstore. But it's also a very thick book that asks me for a serious commitment. And I'm already married.

Now the questions are swirling in my mind: *Which book should I buy? Should I buy a bargain book? A new release? A Christian book? A business book? A classic novel? Should I browse the entire bookstore? Should I buy one book or three for the price of two? Should I read only Christian books? Wait, did I just consider* three *books? What am I thinking? I hardly have the time to read* one *book!*

Inhale. Exhale. Look to the ceiling. Reshelve Dostoyevsky. *Maybe I'll buy a DVD and a pack of gum.*

I have been overwhelmed in a bookstore. Eventually, we will address the practical matters of how to select and read great books. But before we talk about how to pick the right books and how to read them (chaps. 7–15), we need to develop some biblical and theological convictions about books, reading, and bookstores (chaps. 1–6).

Our journey begins in the dust, at the base camp of a desert mountain.

Base Camp

Somewhere around 1450 BC, on a remote Egyptian mountaintop called Mount Sinai, an author wrote something so earth-shaking that the publishing industry has never recovered. It never will.

But to appreciate this moment in literary history let me set the backstory. Several weeks before Mount Sinai appeared on the skyline, God had redeemed his people from slavery. We call this event "the exodus." This exodus was so historic that it became the central salvation event in Old Testament history. Using an army of gnats, flies, locusts, and frogs—and with the help of widespread skin disease, hailstones, a bloodied river, the death of firstborn sons, and the divine power to split the sea—God pried his people out from the tight grip of the Egyptians. Israel was now a liberated people, on a mission to gather around a mountain and serve God together (Exodus 7–12).

The voyage to this mountain was not far, and the wait was not long. In three months Israel had packed up, bolted from Egypt, and arrived at the foot of the mountain—*that* mountain, Mount Sinai (Ex. 19:1).

This chosen mountain may have appeared like all the other mountains of the Sinai Peninsula—red, rocky, dry, and treeless—but it was not like all the rest. This mountain was chosen by God. It was holy. And under the threat of instant death, no man, woman, child, or red heifer dared touch it.

For two days, God's people were to clean house and to purify themselves from all defilements. They were to bathe and wash their clothes and consecrate themselves and prepare to meet with God. On the third day, God would descend, and there they would meet together.

All was calm for two days.

On the morning of the third day, God descended.

God's people rubbed the sleep from their eyes to behold a frightening sight. Tree-bare Mount Sinai was ablaze like a forest fire. The fire raged vertically into the heavens, and the heavens bombarded the mountaintop with thunder and lightning. The foundations of the mountain trembled and quaked. Loose rocks crackled and thudded down the mountainside. A thick, black cloud blanketed the scene.

God's people locked their eyes on the explosive storm. It was hard to look away. Their mouths were wide and speechless, and their desert-cracked skin burned from the heat of the golden flames. Lightning flashes blinked off their clean robes. Fear quickened their hearts.

As the day progressed, the mountain roared with even greater ferocity. The fire grew white-hot, the quaking grew deafening, and lightning continued pounding the peak.

It was the sound and fury of a collision between heaven and earth, "a decisive moment in human history when the celestial and terrestrial realms are brought into panoramic engagement," where "every sort of natural fireworks let loose, so that trembling seizes not only the people but the mountain itself."[1]

Especially now, no one dared approach the mountain. God's people stood at the mountain base, iced with fear. But as the people stepped back in fear, Moses stepped forward in faith (Ex. 20:18). In the face of a blazing mountain covered in dark gloom, a mediator sounded like a very good idea. Some*one* could climb the mountain to represent the people. So Moses climbed into the "thick darkness where God was" (Ex. 20:21).

Moses climbed to meet with God, to worship, and to receive God's words. Moses later recounted the experience in his autobiography:

> When I went up the mountain to receive the tablets of stone, the tablets of the covenant that the LORD made with you, I remained on the mountain forty days and forty nights. I neither ate bread nor drank water. And the Lord gave me the two tablets of stone *written with the finger of God*, and on them were all the words that the LORD had spoken with you on the mountain out of the midst of the fire on the day of the assembly. (Deut. 9:9–10)

Moses climbed back down to the people with two tablets of the Ten Commandments under his arms. These words were permanent, eternal, and etched in stone by the very finger of God.

The One who created the cosmos by the word of his mouth in the beginning, the One who invented human language in Eden, the One who spread languages across the land at Babel, now put pen to paper—or finger to stone—and wrote. To this day, those words can be found in any major bookstore.

Many thousands of books would later be devoted to talking *about* God—proving God, doubting God, explaining God. But these stone tablets held God's words. The day God ran his fingertip over the stone tablets was the day that he forever shaped the world of book publishing.

Written in Stone

In the world of books, the Bible is without equal. We see this in six of its qualities.

The Bible is *inspired*. God is the ultimate and final author of those two tablets, and every other word of Scripture has been breathed out from the mouth of God. The Bible is the product of God's will (2 Tim. 3:16; 2 Pet. 1:20–21).

The Bible is *inerrant*. It is true in everything it teaches. God's Word is like silver that has been smelted sevenfold and is free of all impurities (Ps. 12:6). God's words are always true, because God's words are self-validating. God speaks, and his words shape and resolve what *is* true and good (see Gen. 1:1–31 and John 17:17).

The Bible is *sufficient*. It provides everything we need for faith, salvation, and godly living (2 Tim. 3:15–16).

The Bible is *living and active*. The Bible is composed of living and active words that revive dead hearts, rejoice broken hearts, and feed hungry souls (Matt. 4:4; 1 Cor. 1:21–24; Heb. 4:12; James 1:21).

The Bible is *supreme*. It contains the highest expressions of truth. Combine every book from every culture in human history and pile all those volumes into one vast library, and it cannot trump the supremacy of the life-giving truth in Scripture (1 Cor. 15:3–5).

The Bible offers us a *coherent worldview*. The Bible explains where we came from, where we are going, our biggest problems, and our greatest need. The Bible interprets the realities that affect us—both physical realities that we can see and spiritual realities that we cannot see (see Rom. 4:23–25 and Eph. 6:12).

Scripture is unique. It is eternal. It never contradicts itself. It needs no editing or revision. It is perfect (Ps. 19:7). When all else has disappeared, God's word remains (Isa. 40:7–8). It lacks nothing. And it was all written by the same God who rocked Sinai.

Compost and Granite

The purpose of this book is to study reading from a Christian perspective. So how does Sinai change the way I scan rows of literature at the bookstore? What does a combustible mountaintop have to do with a classic novel by Dostoyevsky, a contemporary novel by Cormac McCarthy, the latest social insights by Malcolm Gladwell, the latest marketing book by Seth Godin, or the latest biography by David McCullough?

Everything.

Scripture is the ultimate grid by which we read every book. Scripture is perfect, sufficient, and eternal. All other books, to some degree, are imperfect, deficient, and temporary. That means that when we pick books from the bookstore shelves, we read those imperfect books in light of the perfect Book, the deficient books in light of the sufficient Book, and the temporary books in light of the eternal Book.

Man-made literature may be inspiring, but it is not divinely inspired—not in the way Scripture is inspired. Man-made literature may be empowered by the Holy Spirit to embody biblical truth, but it's not breathed out by God. Man-made literature may contain truth, goodness, and beauty, but it is also fallible, imperfect, and of temporary value.

We could say that in contrast to God's word all other books are temporary.

All flesh is like grass
    and all its glory like the flower of grass.
The grass withers,
    and the flower falls,

but the word of the Lord remains forever. . . . (1 Pet. 1:24–25; cf. Isa. 40:7–8)

Many authors are average (grass). Other authors are incredibly talented, fruitful, and colorful (flowers). But all authors (grass or flowers) are fragile. Every book that has ascended and descended from the *New York Times* bestseller list is as temporary in value as the green grass under the sweltering summer sun. Authors (including me) and their books (like this one) will return to dust. Man-made literature can help us live more wisely or grow spiritually, but only the God-inspired word is eternal.

Two Genres

Since Moses descended from the mountain with two loose-leaf stones under his arms, all literature can be divided into two genres:

- **Genre A**: *The Bible*. The Bible was written by God through human authors, but it is fully inspired in all its parts. It is the only book that is inspired, inerrant, authoritative, sufficient, and wholly consistent in its worldview.
- **Genre B**: *All other books*. However "inspired" all other literature may be, no matter how "lit" it is with truth, goodness, and beauty, no other book is infallible. All man-made books are hindered to some degree by errors, inconsistencies, and insufficiencies.

These two categories were shaped when God broke into history and ran his finger across a stone tablet. All literature is now divided into two genres—and one soars above the other in importance.

Nineteenth-century preacher Charles Haddon Spurgeon makes this point well:

All other books might be heaped together in one pile and burned with less loss to the world than would be occasioned by the obliteration of a single page of the sacred volume [Scripture]. At their best, all other books are but as gold leaf, requiring acres to find one ounce of the precious metal. But the Bible is solid gold. It contains blocks of gold, mines, and whole caverns of priceless treasure. In the mental wealth of the wisest men there are no jewels like the truths of revelation. The thoughts of men are vanity, low, and groveling at their best. But he who has given us this book has said, "For my thoughts are not your thoughts, neither are your ways my ways, declares the LORD. For as the heavens are higher than the earth, so are my ways higher than your ways and my thoughts than your thoughts" (Isa. 55:8–9). Let it be to you and to me a settled matter that the word of the Lord shall be honored in our minds and enshrined in our hearts. Let others speak as they may. We could sooner part with all that is sublime and beautiful, or cheering and profitable, in *human literature* than lose a single syllable from the *mouth of God.*[2]

Exactly. And if it ever comes down to a decision between losing a page of Scripture or losing a comedy by Shakespeare, we must preserve Scripture.

But of course we aren't forced to part with either of them. We get them *both*—the gold leaf *and* the gold bar. So we must ask more challenging questions: How do we rightly handle the gold leaf (man's literature) now that we have the gold bar (God's Bible)? Does the bar decrease the value of the leaf? Does the bar render the leaf worthless? Or does the bar increase the value of the leaf? Hold this thought, because in chapter 5 I hope to explain how God's sovereign influence can be found in the gold leaf, even in non-Christian books.

The critical point I want you to take from this chapter is this: Before we step into a fully-stocked bookstore, we must be determined to read the *imperfect* in light of the *perfect*, the *deficient* in light of the *sufficient*, the *temporary* in light of the *eternal*, the *groveling* in light of the *transcendent*.

Mount Sinai demands that we distinguish between *temporary* books and the *eternal* Book, between a decomposing paperback from the pen of a sinner and a smoking stone tablet from the finger of God. If we fail to make this distinction, if we fail to prioritize the eternal Word over temporary books, our reading will never be distinctly Christian.

2

Wide-Eyed into the Son

How Personal Sin and the Gospel
Shape Our Literacy

I used one Bible for my entire childhood. And by "used" I mean it provided marginal space for the doodles I sketched during catechism class.

But years later, after she slipped a gold ring on my hand, my wife convinced me to upgrade to a new Bible, one more suitable for an adult. I agreed. We scraped together what cash we had as newlyweds, journeyed to the local Christian bookstore, and walked out with a factory-sealed Bible. It was beautiful.

Within a few hours I was reading the clean Bible and marking all over the pages with a highlighter (a habit I'll explain in chap. 12). My plan was to read the entire New Testament and mark every command from God. It took two weeks. Having so much fun, I continued on to the Old Testament where I found even more commands—lots of commands.

Highlighting all those commands did not change my life overnight. But I did expect my life would begin to change a month later . . .

Or six months later . . .

Or a year later . . .

But nothing changed. My reading did not make me godly. I was powerless to obey the commands simply by reading them.

My plan was clearly defective. I had a problem. And now I see that there *was* a problem—a *big* problem. But it wasn't a mismanufactured Bible, or a failure to read diligently, or the wrong highlighting technique. No, my problem was that I was reading from behind a blindfold.

Blindfolded Saul

God etched words into stone with his finger, and Moses brought the handwritten tablets down from Sinai. But those words alone failed to change lives. The Law itself could offer a list of regulations and it could convict readers of sin, but it could not offer eternal life, it could not change hearts, and it could not generate God-honoring obedience. It was not intended to.

If we fast-forward down the Bible's storyline, we meet a man named Saul, a Jewish scholar. Saul's DNA could be traced back to the men and women who received the tablets written by the finger of God. And Saul devoted his life to the study of those tablets and all the divine literature of Moses (Genesis, Exodus, Leviticus, Numbers, and Deuteronomy). So zealous was he for Moses's writings that Saul persecuted the earliest Christians. He did everything in his power to stop the gospel, to stamp out the church, and to erase from the world any memory of Jesus.

But one day, while traveling along a road, Saul met the glorified Jesus (see Acts 9:1–19). In a blaze of light, Christ knocked Saul into the dust and blinded his eyes. Saul's eyes were physically blinded—but his heart was awakened. Saul became a Christian. Saul became Paul. The raging anti-Christian persecutor became a Jesus-loving Christian. Paul became pivotal in the spread of the gospel. Amazing grace!

This bright encounter removed a blindfold from Paul's eyes. And once his physical eyes recovered, Paul looked around his culture with new perception. He discovered that something was dreadfully wrong. Moses's descendants were blinded to the Savior.

The timing could not have been worse. The long awaited Jewish Savior had arrived right under their noses, but most people—even Paul—had missed him. The promised Savior had come and gone.

But now Paul's eyes were opened to the glory of the Savior. He saw the urgent need for the gospel in the world. His ambitions were focused on spreading this message as widely as possible. The gospel message that he had struggled to destroy was now a message he treasured. And it was a message most people could not see.

Darkened by Sin

This whole story makes me uncomfortable. How could Moses's ancestors, like Paul, have missed their Savior?

We know it was not a problem with their Bibles. The Bible spoke of the coming of a Savior from the early chapters in Genesis, and the Israelites had access to God's written word. It was not a problem of ignoring their Bibles. Every Saturday the Jewish people would gather in synagogues and read together from the Torah—the first five books of the Old Testament written by Moses.[1] This was their practice for centuries.

The problem was much deeper; it was a problem of a sin-induced blindness (Eph. 4:17–19). Sin blinds the heart to the glory of Christ, and when the glory of Christ is not seen, lives remain unchanged.

Here is how the apostle Paul says it:

> For to this day, when they read the old covenant [Moses], that same veil remains unlifted. . . . Yes, to this day whenever Moses is read, a veil lies over their hearts. (2 Cor. 3:14–15)

This is a widespread problem. Because of our sin we are born blind, unable to see the promises of God offered in Christ. And the consequences of our ignorance are spiritually deadly.

Sin blinds our hearts to the true meaning and purpose of the Bible, even if we carry well-highlighted copies in our hands. The problem is not with our Bibles; the problem is with our sinful hearts. Sin darkens and deadens our spiritual perceptions. God must illuminate our hearts. God must act. God must remove the blindfolds.

Unveiled Faces

The sinner's greatest need is to see the light of Christ's glory. But this requires more than a Bible in the hand; it requires an act of God's powerful Spirit in the heart. This act of illumination is so powerful and so obviously the handiwork of God that the fitting metaphor is God's ignition of the sun in our solar system: "For God, who said, 'Let light shine out of darkness,' has shone in our hearts to give the light of the knowledge of the glory of God in the face of Jesus Christ" (2 Cor. 4:6). This is an act of God's sovereign grace. And when he acts, Christians are lit.

When this radiant beauty shines into our hearts, the spiritual veil over our hearts is removed. We behold the Son in all his splendor and life-transforming glory:

> For to this day, when they read the old covenant [Moses], that same veil remains unlifted, *because only through Christ is it taken away.* Yes, to this day whenever Moses is read, a veil lies over their hearts. *But when one turns to the Lord, the veil is removed.* Now the Lord is the Spirit, and where the Spirit of the Lord is, there is freedom. And we all, with *unveiled face, beholding the glory of the Lord*, are being transformed into the same image from one degree of glory to another. For this comes from the Lord who is the Spirit. (2 Cor. 3:14–18)

The removal of a blindfold from the sinner's spiritual eyes is a work of God's sovereign grace. And once the blindfold is removed, the purposes of God's law and commandments become clear. The smoldering tablets of Commandments were not intended to serve as a mere social standard, but as a tutor to lead us by the hand to see the depth of our own sin and to see the glory of the Savior (Gal. 3:23–29). If we can see these realities, it is because God has acted upon us and unveiled our faces.

This unveiling transforms how we read books.

It is possible to have a photographic memory and the capacity to remember everything you read with flawless recollection. But if the Spirit of God has not reached down and unwrapped the black veil from over from your heart, eternal truth will be pitch darkness to you. You may see words on a cold page of paper, but you will not feel the warm brightness of Christ's glory. And you will not experience eternal life.[2]

The day you are *lit*, the day God removes the veil from your heart and reveals the glory of his Son to you, is an experience that will radically change your life. And beholding the glory of Christ will transform how you read books—every book.

My Unveiling

A little over a year after I began my hunt for every command in the Bible, God unveiled my face. This was odd because while my physical eyesight is pathetic, I thought my spiritual vision was 20/20. I was "baptized" in diapers and "confirmed" to be a Christian in my teens. I happily attended church each week and read my Bible with a highlighter in hand. All the signs indicated that I was a model Christian man. But I wasn't. I wasn't a Christian at all. I was blindfolded.

One Sunday morning (Sept. 9, 1999) God removed that blindfold. Sitting in a church in Lincoln, Nebraska, with my well-highlighted Bible on my lap, I listened as a faithful preacher expounded Luke 18:9–14. He carefully and clearly explained the difference between a broken sinner (a tax collector) and a self-righteous Bible highlighter (a Pharisee). The grace of God acted upon me. The veil was lifted. And in a moment I discovered my problem: I was a Pharisee. Functionally, I had pushed Christ aside and attempted to atone for my sin through personal obedience to God's commands. I was blind to the glory of Christ.

On that morning, I was broken over my sin. I discovered that my life pursuits were hopeless without Christ. My self-righteous attempts to please God were dashed to the ground. I could never accomplish the task. That morning I turned to the Lord for the first time, the Holy Spirit removed my blindfold, and I beheld the glorious person and work of Christ.

Like a light switched on in a dark room, Christ's glory became visible to me for the first time. And the view was stunning!

I began to see that Jesus Christ had eternally existed. He is the creator of all things and the origin of every particle in the cosmos! He now sustains that creation, rules over it, and will one day re-create it.

I can now see Jesus as God-incarnate, the Word made flesh. He stooped low to take the form of man and dwelt among us for thirty-three years. He walked in our shoes. He shouldered a life of sorrows. He was tempted by every sin, but he remained steadfast at every step—faithful, sinless, regretless. During those years, Jesus opened the eyes of the blind, stood the paralyzed on their feet, and raised the dead. He preached deliverance to sinners who were trapped in wickedness and preached forgiveness to the religious who were entangled in self-righteousness.

I can now see Jesus, the anointed Savior-King. He is the one mediator between holy God and sinful man. He humbled himself to the point of death, even death on a cross. There he was suspended in the air between heaven and earth on a tree, rejected by sinful men, and forsaken by a holy God. Here in this lonely mockery, Jesus reconciled man and God. Jesus *became* sin. My sin was charged to him. He bore my guilt and died my spiritual death.

He took up flesh and blood only to have his flesh torn and his blood drained. Through his atoning sacrifice, his righteousness is credited to me. I have been justified, pardoned, and fully accepted by a holy God. By that blood I have been saved from the slavery to sin, from the curse of the Law, from the power of Satan, from the judgment of God, and from the dead end of my empty self-righteousness. I have become God's child. God has become my Father. Jesus has become my Friend. Jesus is forever my High Priest, who has opened the curtain into God's presence. He now intercedes for me, ensuring that nothing ever separates me from God's love.

I can now see Jesus raised. Jesus was raised from the dead as a claim of victory over sin, death, and Satan. His resurrection inaugurated the new creation. His blood inaugurated the new covenant.

I can now see Jesus, the head of his body, the church. Every Christian is united together in him, all of us drawing our identity and spiritual strength from him. He is our life, our wisdom, our righteousness, our sanctification, and our redemption.

I can now see Jesus ascended. Jesus returned to the presence of his Father, where he sits on his throne and reigns as the King of kings. One day he will return to earth with a sword in his hand to strike down the wicked and to trample them in the winepress of the fury of God's wrath. He is coming to judge the living and the dead. And he will finally rid the earth forever of all sin, all calamity, all death, all disease, and all the temptations and lies and deception of Satan.

I can now see the magnificence of our Savior. He is fully God and fully man. He is the Lion and the Lamb—the Sovereign and the Sufferer. He is the Prophet, Priest, and King—speaking, dying, and reigning. He is Light to the blind, Health to the sinfully sick, Strength to the spiritually weak, Food for the spiritually famished, Joy for the sorrowful heart, Comfort for the despised, Deliverance for lost souls, Drink for the thirsty soul, and Triumph for the abused. He is my Savior, my Shepherd, my Friend, my Lord, my Life, my Way, my End.

Jesus is worthy of our time, our worship, and our devotion. The sight of Christ's glory permanently changed my life.

And it forever changed how I read books.

The Mind of Christ

Faith in Jesus brings with it a critically important benefit for the Christian reader—discernment. Discernment is the ability to do three things: the ability to "test everything," to "hold fast what is good," and to "abstain from every form of evil" (1 Thess. 5:21–22). It is the skill of comparing what we hear or read with God's Word to determine its authenticity according to God's revealed truth. Discernment is critical for evaluating everything said *inside* a church building, and it is equally critical for evaluating life experienced *outside* the church context. We need discernment to hear sermons, to watch movies, and to read books. Discernment protects the church, and discernment protects our hearts.

The grace of God in our lives is the foundation of all our discernment. Christian discernment begins when the veil is removed and we behold the glory of Christ. When this happens, we truly become "spiritual" and thus possess "the mind of Christ" (1 Cor. 2:15–16). We now read, think, and live our lives by the light of the spiritual truths of the gospel. We are now gospel-minded. And with the "mind of Christ" we are now capable of reading with discernment. We can test every book that we read—to treasure what is true, good, and pure in God's eyes, and to reject what is evil (Rom. 12:2).

Christ is essential to all discernment, because he is the standard of all truth and the remedy to all error (Col. 2:8). Christ must be at the center of our lives if we will ever read with discernment. Christ will only be at the center of our lives if our eyes behold his glory. We will only behold his glory if the veil is removed from our eyes.

Once God enlightens our spiritual eyes, we can read books for the spiritual benefit of our souls—whether it's the Ten Commandments, a thick systematic theology, the poems of John Donne, C. S. Lewis's The Chronicles of Narnia, or a microbiology textbook. To read any book for eternal benefit, we must behold the glory of Christ. His glory lies at the bottom of all sound knowledge and learning.[3]

Reading for Communion

Having the "mind of Christ" will not make you brilliantly smart. I wish my conversion had transformed me into a brilliant astrophysicist or a world-class neurosurgeon! It didn't. Beholding the glory of Christ *did* transform my life, my worldview, and my desire to read. But my conversion *did not* give me a photographic memory, it *did not* merit me an honorary doctorate from MIT, and it *did not* boost my brain capacity to Vulcan-strength.

In fact, I did not then (and have not since) learned everything there is to know about God. Of course I didn't. In fact, conversion does not promise that I will know more information about God than some who are not Christians. Puritan theologian John Owen wrestled with this fact when he wrote:

> The difference between the knowledge of believers and unbelievers is not so much a difference in the *matter* of their knowledge but in the *manner* of knowing. Unbelievers, some of them, know more about God, his perfections, and his will, than many believers do; but they know nothing as they ought, nothing in a right manner, nothing spiritually and savingly, nothing with a holy and heavenly light. The excellence of a believer is not that he has a large grasp of

things, but that what he does grasp, which may be very little, he sees it in the light of the Spirit of God, in a saving, soul-transforming light; and this is that which gives us communion with God.[4]

Having been unveiled to the cross of Christ does not make us smart. But it does change how we read and learn. It does not make learning easier. But it does mean we can discern between what is temporal and short-lived and what is weighty and eternal. The true difference in our knowledge is not found in *what* we know but *why* we know it. Christians learn to commune.

Christian book reading is never a solitary experience, but an open invitation to commune with God. By opening a book we can stop talking and we begin listening. We can turn from the distractions of life. We can focus our minds. Sometimes we can even lose all sense of time. Although it's difficult to protect, this reading environment can be the atmosphere that sustains the life of interaction with God.

Owen is speaking here of reading the Bible, but I will argue throughout this book that there is an eternal dimension to everything we read—whether we read theology, poetry, novels, business books, or textbooks. As Christians, we read all of our books illuminated by God and in communion with him. Gleaning facts and information is not the highest purpose of reading. Reading can be ultimately a means to eternally benefit our soul. And this benefit does not hinge upon how smart we are, upon how many books we read each year, or upon how much information we retain. We tap into the eternal value of literature when we read in the presence of God, unveiled to the glory of our Savior.

Dropping Blindfolds in the Dust

Looking back, it is obvious why my highlighted Bible seemed powerless to change my life. I was the problem. I was reading in the dark, blindfolded by my own sin and self-righteousness. I diligently studied the Bible, but without profit and comprehension, because I could see nothing more on the page than a list of commands to obey. I was blind to the Savior's glory, and therefore the Bible made no sense to me. I now see that Jesus Christ is the heart of the entire Bible and without him it makes no sense. Or as Martin Luther said, "To possess Scripture without knowing Christ, is to have no Scripture."[5]

After all that time highlighting Scripture, I had no Scripture, and that is a frightening thought. But this experience helped me to understand the profound impact the gospel makes on how we read books. Without Christ, we remain blind to the most profound and glorious realities of the universe, we cannot understand the Bible rightly, and we cannot see and delight in the truth, goodness, and beauty of God that we read. And we cannot use our reading as a means of enjoying the presence of God.

I learned valuable lessons from that new Bible I purchased as a newlywed. The gift of literacy is more profound than merely mastering literacy techniques, improving comprehension, and learning to speed-read. Fundamentally, literacy is a spiritual discipline that must overcome the spiritual darkness that veils us. If we ever hope to spiritually benefit from our reading, the Holy Spirit must intrude upon our lives and remove our blindfolds so that we can behold the radiant glory of Jesus Christ (John 1:9).

Once we see His glory, our literacy—*how* we read books—is permanently and forever changed.

3

Reading Is Believing

Savoring Books in an Eye-Candy Culture

Imagine reading a newspaper with no color and no pictures. Until the Civil War, newspapers were like this—line after line, paragraph after paragraph, column after column of simple black text. Not only were the papers bland and boring, they were reproduced very slowly, and this meant readership was limited.

All this changed in the 1860s and 1870s. Publishers discovered new ways to incorporate images into print, and they innovated a way to increase the speed of printing. Newspapers began reproducing visual images to a growing audience of image-hungry subscribers.

These innovations pioneered what Daniel Boorstin has labeled the "graphic revolution," a revolution that would forever change the way Americans receive their news.[1] In his landmark book *Amusing Ourselves to Death,* sociologist Neil Postman explains the consequences:

> The new focus on the image undermined traditional definitions of information, of news, and, to a large extent, of reality itself. First in billboards, posters, and advertisements, and later in such "news" magazines and papers as *Life*, *Look*, the New York *Daily Mirror* and

Daily News, the pictures forced exposition into the background, and in some instances obliterated it altogether. By the end of the nineteenth century, advertisers and newspapermen had discovered that a picture was not only worth a thousand words, but, where sales were concerned, was better. For countless Americans, seeing, not reading, became the basis for believing.[2]

Today we live in the tidal wave of the graphic revolution. No serious newspaper would dare publish *without* pictures. In fact, writes David Wells, "The cultural mantle has passed from the users of words to the makers of images."[3] And most of us have only known a world dominated by images: glossy magazines, wide billboards, corporate icons, realistic video games, 3D movies, and high-definition TVs. Images now provide "the daily nutrient of our sensory experience, our thought process, our feelings, and our ideology."[4]

This trend is troubling because the immediate appeal of visual entertainment is at odds with the gradual unveiling of literary treasure. Entertainment is passive and easy; books require an active mind and diligence. Books typically get ignored.

In this chapter I want to think about images and books and life. What will we lose if we ignore books? And what will we lose if we fill our lives for the next the twenty years with sitcoms, movies, ESPN, video games, and the Internet? What will we gain if we fill our lives for the next twenty years with disciplined reading?

This chapter is about images and books, but more fundamentally it's about the trajectory of your life. Before we submit our complete attention to this graphic revolution, let's think about what's at stake.

Relics

If the Old Testament history is a play, pagan idolatry is the scenery on the stage where Israel acted out its history. Long before a laser hit the back of a whirling DVD or an image was digitized on a memory card, God's people were encircled by cultures that petrified their gods and goddesses.

In those cultures, small household gods were collected and feared. Images of the gods were painted on the walls, cut into metal, carved out of logs, and propped up in the fields. Grown men pursued divine blessing and worldly prosperity by pressing their lips to the cold stone mouth of coldhearted statues. Deceived parents were willing to offer the blood of their own children to pacify the gods (Ezek. 16:20–37). So pervasive were the images and idols that the Bible often speaks in shorthand of pagan nations as those who "worship wood and stone" (Ezek. 20:32; see Dan. 5:4, 23; Rev. 9:20).

By contrast, God planned to lead his people through this world of visual idols by words from his own lips—in language, through his revealed Word.[5] But the temptation to follow the pagan cultures and to mold God into a golden image was an indulgence the Israelites found impossible to resist.

By the time Moses's sandals hit the base of Mount Sinai with God's commandments under his arms, God's people had collected their golden earrings, melted them in a fire, and cast a golden calf (Exodus 32). The adornment of the ear was sacrificed in order to create an image pleasing to the eye. The ear (the receiver of God's word) was plundered for the eye (the receiver of the image). The irony is striking.

It didn't take long for Israel to abandon God's Word in favor of a culturally-shaped image.

The Second Commandment

At Sinai, God prohibited Israel from creating and worshiping images of himself. In the second commandment, God wrote this with his finger on the stone tablet:

> You shall not make for yourself a carved image, or any likeness of anything that is in heaven above, or that is in the earth beneath, or that is in the water under the earth. You shall not bow down to them or serve them, for I the LORD your God am a jealous God. . . . (Ex. 20:4–5)

But why *this* command? It seems counterintuitive and counterproductive, or at least excessive. Aren't images just another form of communicating truth, perhaps even more effective than words? Cannot images be a means of educating the illiterate? Besides, wouldn't carved images of God prove helpful in contextualizing and winning the hearts of the nations more familiar with visible images of their gods?

God's command is protective. A culture that must express its gods in visual images cannot know God accurately. And a culture that cannot know God accurately cannot communicate God's substance truthfully. For the Christian, media forms carry ethical consequences.

God's ban upon images of himself would have sounded absurd to people in the Ancient Near East. In fact, this ban distinguished Israel from the other nations. God's people would center their devotion upon the word of God, not upon images of a god.

At one level, this word/image tension is a battle for our hearts. God wants us to listen to him, to love him, to experience his presence, to interpret what we feel and what we see in light of his Word. He wants us to hope for a world unseen. He wants his truth and his Word to govern our hearts. Language is the basis of our relationship with God, and a deeply personal means to experience him. Therefore *how* God is communicated is a matter of serious concern.

Exiled

Fast-forward four decades past Sinai. Israel now stands on the cusp of the Promised Land, and Moses nears the end of his life. God's nomadic people are ready to begin their conquest of the Promised Land.

At this watershed moment in Israel's history, Moses warns the people of their lust for visual idols. He points them back to Sinai and reminds them that when God spoke from the mountain they "saw no form," rather, "there was only a voice" (Deut. 4:12). God's visual concealment provided the basis for Moses to warn the people about the lure of the carved images (4:15–30). If the people closed their ears to his Word and devoted themselves to idols, God would judge them. Moses's warning was clear:

> When you father children and children's children, and have grown old in the land, if you act corruptly by making a *carved image* in the form of anything, and by doing what is evil in the sight of the LORD your God, so as to provoke him to anger, I call heaven and earth to

witness against you today, that you will soon utterly perish from the land that you are going over the Jordan to possess. You will not live long in it, but will be utterly destroyed. And the LORD will scatter you among the peoples, and you will be left few in number among the nations where the LORD will drive you. And there you will serve *gods of wood and stone, the work of human hands, that neither see, nor hear, nor eat, nor smell.* But from there you will seek the LORD your God and you will find him, if you search after him with all your heart and with all your soul. When you are in tribulation, and all these things come upon you in the latter days, you will return to the LORD your God and obey *his voice.* (Deut. 4:25–30)

Moses's warning was tragically prophetic. Centuries later (722 BC), Israel was pillaged by Assyria, and God's people were carried off into exile. Why? Because "they abandoned all the *commandments* of the LORD their God, and made for themselves metal *images*..." (2 Kings 17:16). Israel traded God's word for images.

The Long War against Words

In part, the Old Testament is God's struggle to lead a language-centered people through the allurements of an image-dominated world. And it makes me ask: are we safe?

Today's images may not appear in the form of a Baal statue or a man puckered up to a stone idol, but the temptations remain. In a culture so dominated by televised images, writes church historian Carl Trueman, the value of the written word easily erodes: "Paralleling the rise of the television-driven visual culture has been the collapse in confidence in language."[6] The contemporary cultural attraction to video images over language, to the aesthetic over the cerebral, is what Trueman calls "the long war against words."[7]

But the tension is not simply between the value of words and the value of images. Both language and visual images are valuable. The concern is whether Christians (like us) will be patient enough to find meaning embedded in words, or if we will grow content with the superficial pleasures offered to us in the rapidly shifting images in our culture.

Language, Images, and Meaning

Words and images are both valuable because words and images both communicate meaning. But they do not communicate in the same way, or to the same degree. In fact, language is the more precise of the two.

Ideally *words* and *images* should be kept together. Words help explain images. Images help illustrate words. But for the purpose of illustration, I want to take a moment to separate words and images and to contrast the value of *language* and *images* as carriers of meaning. In four ways, words are better suited to communicate precise meaning.

1. Language Best Captures the Meaning of Visible Realities

As I write, relief work has kicked into overtime after the catastrophic earthquake in the nation of Haiti. Death toll estimates have risen to over one hundred thousand. Dump trucks heave bodies into mass graves. The scene is inconceivable. I flip through the graphic images of the destruction online and pray for the people.

The disturbing images help me to see the chaos of the situation. But what this earthquake *means* for the people in streets, and for the nation as a whole, cannot be captured by images. I see a photo of a man weeping. But I cannot tell *why* he weeps. Does he weep because of the shock? Does he weep over the pain in his bloodied arm? Does he weep at the loss of his home? Does he weep at the loss of his child? Does he weep at the news that his child, once thought dead, is alive and healthy? I cannot tell from the picture whether the man weeps because of grief or relief. Without a caption, without an interview of the man, without more detail, the picture cannot provide any more meaning than what we can see on the surface of the image itself.

As a viewer of the images, I need words and explanation to interpret the images accurately. Once I receive the words, the pictures are given a richer and deeper meaning. Pictures can raise questions in my mind and give me an appetite to read and understand what I see, but the image itself offers me very limited meaning.

In contrast, I reach for the writings of Puritan Anne Bradstreet and examine her poem, "Some Verses upon the Burning of Our House"

(1666). There Bradstreet expresses the heart-wrenching experience of looking at the smoldering rubble of a house that represented her home, her memories, and her life's work. I hold the poem next to the images from Haiti. In the photos from Haiti I see the appearance of tragedy. In Bradstreet's poem I feel the heavy weight of tragedy upon the soul.

This contrast between a *picture* from Haiti and a *poem* from Bradstreet is explained in the words of Os Guinness: "The world of sight, the world of the eye, cannot take us *beyond* what is shown. Because sight can only go so far, it takes words and thought to give the real truth and meaning behind what is seen."[8]

Words are a more precise way of communicating the meaning behind the images of our world. This explains why old silent movies needed text slides, why new movies need writers and dialogue, and why newspaper photographs call for captions. Language brings precision and clarity of meaning to what we see with our eyes.

2. Language Best Communicates Invisible Realities

What is *real* extends far deeper than what we can see. Our holy God is real. Our sinful guilt before him is real. The justifying grace of God in the gospel is real. Our Savior is real. Heaven is real. Angels are real. But for now these realities are invisible.

Images do capture stunning scenes and events, but words take you by the hand down to the depths of the human soul and up to the heights of an unseen eternity. This is why what we can learn about God by looking at his visible creation (general revelation) is limited. We need his word (special revelation) to help "see" what is invisible.

This point is illustrated in the period of history leading up to the Protestant Reformation. The Roman Catholic Church had attempted to teach religious truth to the illiterate through icons, paintings, and sculptures. Having refused to teach the Bible in the common language of the people, they turned to images, insisting that "images are the books of the unlearned." But this idea was reckless, said the Reformers. John Calvin pointed out that while those images could capture life experiences and beauty, they were unable to teach eternal truth.[9] In fact, the images only perpetuated the ignorance of the illiterate to eternal truth! What the people needed was the preaching of God's Word in their own language. Only words sufficiently carried the invisible realities of God. Viewed from this angle, the Reformation was "a recovery of the biblical centrality of words."[10]

We are often told that *seeing is believing*. But Jesus says, "Blessed are those who *have not seen* and yet have believed" (John 20:29). And Peter writes, "Though you *have not seen* him, you love him. Though you *do not now see* him, you believe in him and rejoice with joy that is inexpressible and filled with glory" (1 Pet. 1:8). Jesus was visible, and will again be visible to us. Now he is invisible. Revelation (words) makes it possible for us to gaze into the unseen and *see* him by faith.[11]

Visual images are not meaningless. In fact some knowledge of God—his existence, his goodness, his creative power—is visible in creation (Ps. 19:2; Rom. 1:18–20). But when it comes to understanding the invisible realities of God, we must have revelation, we must have language, and we must have words.

3. Language Best Informs Our Eternal Hope
God designed language to teach us about saving faith, eternal hope, and divine promises. Because language enables us to believe in the unseen, language makes faith possible. "Faith attaches itself to a thing that is still an utter nothing, and waits until everything comes about," writes Martin Luther. "It is a knowledge and wisdom of darkness and nothingness, that is, of things which it has not experienced and are unseen and almost impossible."[12] Faith requires language.

God's words and promises deliver hope to our souls. These words equip Christians to rest on their deathbeds, as they cling in their hearts to spiritual realities that they have never held in their hands or seen with their eyes (Heb. 11:13).

Images can capture our attention, move our emotions, and provide us with a lifetime of God-glorifying aesthetic delight. But we must have revelation and language to receive divine promises.

4. Language Makes Worldview Possible
An image may be worth a thousand words, but it can do little more than capture the appearance of an isolated event. One thousand

images stitched together may reveal a panoramic landscape, but they cannot capture a worldview.

Because images capture the appearance of fragmented places and events in the world, our lives cannot find context through images. A photograph cannot be taken out of context, writes Postman, because "a photograph does not require one. In fact the point of photography is to isolate images from context, so as to make them visible in a different way." He writes, "Photography recreates the world as a series of idiosyncratic events. There is no beginning, middle, or end in a world of photographs. . . . The world is atomized."[13]

The opposite of fragmentation is cohesion, and cohesion is vital to the Christian worldview. With language we can learn or express ideas, abstractions, the internal, and the unseen. Only language makes it possible for us to develop and understand and communicate a cohesive worldview (the focus of the next chapter).

At this point some will object. Don't words have the power to damage and destroy? Yes, of course. Literature can be twisted into pornography for the imagination that is as dangerous and as powerful as pornographic images. Words can also be twisted into damaging lies, or malicious slander, or hateful propaganda.

But my point here is a simple one: as a word-centered people we must learn to prize language in a visually-dominated world. If our hearts prioritize images over language, our hunger for books will erode.

Shattering Snakes

Images and visual arts are not superficial or unnecessary. Art is a powerful tool to complement language. This is clear in the conversion testimony of Peter Hitchens, brother of famous atheist Christopher Hitchens. For Peter, viewing the realistically painted men and women fleeing from God's judgment in Rogier van der Weyden's work *The Damned Plunging into Hell* (fifteenth century) was so alarming that he converted from atheism.[14] In this case the truth of God's judgment had already been planted in his religious childhood, and those truths surfaced when he beheld the painting.

Art may be powerless to save sinners, but it is a powerful tool to remind us of truth and to illustrate truth.

The Damned Plunging into Hell

My conversion story contains no artwork, but I do value images. Photography is a favorite hobby of mine. I appreciate my artistically gifted friends, and I value their God-honoring work. I enjoy walking with my wife through the National Art Gallery in DC, watching a Pixar-animated film in 3D with my family, and reading beautifully illustrated picture books with my children.

More importantly, Scripture tells us that God appreciates visual art. In the Old Testament, God filled men with artistic skill in order to decorate both the tabernacle and the temple with beauty (Ex. 31:1–11; 1 Kings 6:1–7:51). And I believe God continues to bless the church with Spirit-filled artists who are called to adorn God's truth with beautiful ornamentation for us to enjoy.

We must, however, remain aware that since sin was introduced into the world, visual images are easily corrupted.

Take the story of Moses's bronze serpent (Num. 21:4–9). At one point in the desert wanderings, deadly snakes attacked God's grumbling people. Many of the people were bitten and died. After Moses repented for the people's grumbling, God instructed Moses to shape a bronze serpent impaled on a pole. When those who were dying from the poison merely looked at the bronze image in faith, God healed them. So what later happened to that bronze serpent? It was given a name, it was enshrined, and it was worshiped. It became an object of idolatrous lust. Hezekiah, a wise king of Israel, later busted the bronze serpent into pieces (2 Kings 18:4).

Image worship is the sinner's tendency. We are prone to revere images that are beautiful, and then to misuse them. We can make idols out of anything visual: crucifixes, icons of the saints, images of Mary, images of Jesus, the profile of a potato chip, the outline created by the water stain on a wall, etc. The danger is rooted in our hearts. Our tendency is to worship bronze and to ignore the God who heals the dying.

Nevertheless, when language takes its proper priority in our lives, we can appreciate images and art as a source of God-glorifying beauty.

Beatifical

We were created to *see* Jesus. But look around, and you'll discover that Jesus isn't visible.[15] Today we "see" Christ's glory *by faith* in the words of Scripture. But a day approaches when all Christians will see *with their physical eyes* the glory that radiates from the person of Jesus Christ (Matt. 5:8; John 17:24; 1 Cor. 13:12; Rev. 22:4).

And on the glorious day when we *see* Jesus, our temporary faith in Jesus will be replaced by an eternal enjoyment of the sight of Jesus. What we've *read* about God will be reconciled to what we *see* of God.

But we must wait for that day. We do not yet live in the age of the eye; we live in the age of the ear, we live in the age of revelation and promises and books.[16] The implanted desire to *see* God will be continually frustrated. For now we sing, "Lord, haste the day when my faith shall be sight."

So the point of this chapter is simple: the *difficult work* required to benefit from books is at odds with the *immediate appeal* of images.

As Christians living in an image-saturated world, we must guard our conviction about the vital importance of words and language. For it is words and language that best communicate meaning.

In a world so easily satisfied with images, it's too easy to waste our lives watching mindless television and squandering our free time away with entertainment. We have a higher calling. God has called us to live our lives by faith and not by sight—and this can mean nothing less than committing our lives to the pursuit of language, revelation, and great books.

4

Reading from across the Canyon

How a Biblical Worldview Equips Us to Benefit from Books

I was born with an insatiable hunger for stories. Give me tales of rags-to-riches, self-discovery, and the triumph of good over evil. Give me ancient stories about kings and queens and warfare. And when the historical accounts run dry, give me myths and fables of dragons and knights and princesses.

Stories arrest us. Parents use stories to capture the attention of active children. Preachers use stories to capture the attention of sleepy adults. The promise of a good story will draw us into the movie theater, the playhouse, and the bookstore. We are people born with an endless appetite for narratives.

But stories do more than entertain and inspire us. Stories make claims about the world in which we live. Stories can also inform the mind and edify the soul. If we have the right story, we can learn a lot about our world, our problems, and even ourselves. Writes Neil Postman, "Human beings require stories to give meaning to the facts of their existence."[1] He is not talking about the value of bedtime stories. He is talking about the human need for a single Story, a Story so big that it can make sense of the story that is our life. Scripture provides us with this Story.

The general plot of the biblical Story hangs on the progress of *creation, fall, redemption,* and *restoration.* Within this plot we learn propositional truths that inform us about the activity of God, the condition of our world, the dignity of humanity, the sin in our hearts, the work of the Savior, the return of our Savior, and the restoration of nature. The Bible answers important personal questions like: Where do I come from? Who am I? What went wrong with this world? What went wrong with me? What can be done about it? And what can we expect in the future? Answers to each of these questions are found in the pages of Scripture, and these answers will shape how we view ourselves, others, and the world in which we live. When these truths operate in our minds, we are living by a Christian *worldview.* And it is impossible to be a discerning reader of books without first understanding the Christian worldview.

Worldview by Autopsy

So how do we develop a biblical worldview? Our worldview convictions are best formed by autopsy, by seeing things with our own eyes. Like a coroner slicing the flesh of a cold corpse to examine the cause of death with his or her own eyes, constructing a Christian worldview should be informed by the direct study of an open Bible with our own eyes.

Our worldview convictions are too important to be based upon secondary literature. Although it is common to find a Judeo-Christian influence in literature, literature that features a robust and functional biblical worldview is less prevalent. For example, the writings of William Shakespeare were obviously impacted by the Geneva Bible (1560) and *The Book of Common Prayer* (1559). Yet for all the value of reading and studying Shakespeare's works, it would be difficult to develop a biblical worldview from reading his works—or from any fictional literature alone.

By reading Scripture under the illuminating grace of the Holy Spirit, we develop biblical convictions that make us competent to discern truth from lies, goodness from evil, and beauty from ugliness. Before we can be discerning, we must be informed by a direct study of Scripture.

Worldview Work

Developing a biblical worldview is labor-intensive, but the result is a discerning mind that is essential if we will benefit from books. If we fail here, we will be flooded with worldviews of other authors and be quickly overwhelmed, confused, and frustrated. On the other hand, firm biblical convictions will make it possible for us to benefit from a broad array of literature by Christians and non-Christians alike. More about that in a minute.

First, let's look at seven critical truths in Scripture. In this section I want to turn your attention to the Bible, beginning with the most fundamental question of all.

Does God Exist?

From its first sentence, the Bible assumes God's existence. God existed before the world existed (Ps. 90:2). He exists in three persons—Father, Son, and Holy Spirit (2 Cor. 13:14). When it comes to his influence, God is sovereign and he does whatever he pleases (Ps. 115:3). God's pure holiness is beyond all comparison (1 Sam. 2:2).

God is *self-subsisting*. He was not created. And although we require everything from him, God needs nothing from us (Acts 17:24–25).

God is *self-sufficient*. God does not plug in to recharge. He does not eat. God draws his life from himself (John 5:26). Just as God was never born into existence, so God will never die. Because he is self-sufficient, God will live on "forever and ever" (Rev. 4:10).

God is *all-sufficient*. God is the source of all power. He is also the source and supply of every temporal and eternal blessing we will ever enjoy (Pss. 16:2; 104; Matt. 5:45; 1 Tim. 6:17).

God is the Supreme Being in the universe and the source of all truth, goodness, and beauty in creation.

Does Truth Exist?

Yes, it does. The Bible is absolutely true, according to Jesus (John 17:17). Jesus Christ himself is the living Word of God (John 1:1–5).

"And we know that the Son of God has come and has given us understanding, so that we may know him who is *true*; and we are in him who is *true*, in his Son Jesus Christ. He is the *true* God and eternal life" (1 John 5:20). Jesus Christ *is* eternal truth. He came to bear witness to the truth (John 18:37). When faced with the question, "What is truth?" Jesus stands as the silent answer (v. 38). He is the point where God, man, words, meaning, reality, and truth all converge. Truth not only exists, truth lives and breathes and speaks and dies and rises and saves and reigns eternally.

Where Did Our World Come From?

The universe was conceived in God's imagination and birthed by his spoken word (Genesis 1–2; Heb. 11:3; Rev. 4:11). At the beginning, God's creation existed in perfect *shalom*, a harmony that resulted from the "webbing together of God, humans, and all creation in justice, fulfillment, and delight."[2] Christ was the architect of creation, and to this day he now holds the atoms of the universe together by the word of his power (Col. 1:15–17; Heb. 1:3).

What Went Wrong with Our World?

Sin. Sin is lawlessness, rebellion against the commands of God (1 John 3:4). Sin was introduced into God's perfect creation in the garden of Eden (Genesis 3). From that day God's perfect peace, his *shalom*, was broken. Sin corrupted creation, and it corrupted the relationships between mankind to God and mankind to one another. Death appeared. The harmony of the original creation turned to chaos.

For this first sin, God judged his creation and subjected the world to frustration, futility, vanity, and emptiness (Gen. 3:8–19; Ecclesiastes). The whole creation now groans to be freed from the curse brought upon it by humankind's sin (Rom. 8:20–22).

In Adam every man, woman, and child is sinful from the point of conception. The impulse to disobey God and to suppress God's truth flows naturally from our hearts (Rom. 1:18–32). We naturally hurt each other and, even worse, we are naturally alienated from God (Ephesians 2). This alienation sentences sinners to physical and spiritual death (Gen. 2:7; 3:19; Rom. 5:12–21; 6:23; I Cor. 15:20–26). The human alienation from God breeds thinking (and the publishing of books) that is hostile toward God and ignorant of his true character (Romans 1–2; 12:2; I John 2:15–17). The harmony between God and his creation is fractured by sin.

Bible scholar D. A. Carson captures it well: "In sum, we find ourselves fighting the Bible's entire story line if we do not recognize that our deepest need is to be reconciled to God (cf. 2 Cor. 5:11–21)."[3] Likewise, our story will not make sense until we see that our greatest personal problem is enmity against God, and our greatest personal need is reconciliation with God.

Who Are We?

But who exactly are we? Humankind—male and female—is the crown jewel of God's creation, created to find eternal pleasure in God (Deut. 13:4; Ps. 16:11). God originally created man from the dust of the ground and the living breath of God (Gen. 2:7). Men and women image God, reflecting God in our various faculties (mind, will, emotions, reason, personality), and in our authority over creation (Gen. 1:26–27). Men and women are spiritually equal, but are each given different, complementary gender-based roles (I Cor. 11:3).

Even after sin entered into creation, mankind retained something of the image of God. The Bible reconciles the mystery of human splendor and wickedness. Man is complex. Man is a paradox. Man is both "the glory and the garbage of the universe."[4] "We human beings are a mystery to ourselves," writes theologian Daniel Migliore. "We are rational and irrational, civilized and savage, capable of deep friendship and murderous hostility, free and in bondage, the pinnacle of creation and its greatest danger. We are Rembrandt and Hitler, Mozart and Stalin, Antigone and Lady Macbeth, Ruth and Jezebel."[5] Evidence for the glory of man, and for the sinful garbage of man, can be found throughout Scripture.

No matter how rational, civilized, friendly, and glorious, we are all sinners and we are all guilty for our sin before a holy God and await his eternal punishment (Matt. 25:46; 2 Thess. 1:5–12).

What Is the Solution to Our Dilemma?

Jesus Christ is the solution. The solution to sin is found in his birth, his life, his death, his burial, his resurrection, and his ascension into heaven. No fact is more important (1 Cor. 15:3–5).

Although it's a bit ironic, we discover our greatest problem when we see the gospel solution. In the gospel of Jesus Christ we see our greatest need.

In Christ, the power of sin is broken, the powers of death and Satan are defeated, and the guilt of sinners is covered (Hebrews 10). Only through Christ can sinners be reconciled to God (John 14:6; Ephesians 2; Col. 1:19–23).

In Christ are found all the treasures of wisdom and knowledge for eternal life (Col. 2:2–3). Humans find their purpose and meaning in Christ. Christ is the way, the truth, and the life (John 14:6). He is the One who nourishes the sinner's soul with the living water and living bread (John 4:7–15; 6:22–59).

God is now removing blindfolds and bringing spiritual life to sinners where there was only spiritual deadness (Ezek. 36:25–27). In Christ, the image of God in humanity is being restored from the corruption caused by sin (Col. 3:10). And in Christ, spiritual life and the promise of eternal physical life are given to sinners who believe (1 Corinthians 15). Christ's substitutionary death for us is the grand solution to the grand human dilemma.

Where Is History Headed?

God is restoring his creation (Acts 3:21). He will re-create the creation that has been broken by sin, and will make all things new (Rev. 21:5). Christ will one day return to destroy evil forever and to restore the perfect *shalom* to his creation (Isa. 11:1–9).

The process has begun, and our world is in a dusty incomplete state of remodeling. Through the gospel of Jesus Christ, God is now chipping sin from sinners (Heb. 12:1). The work of re-creation has begun; the new creation has been inaugurated (2 Cor. 5:17; Gal. 6:15).

Believers join with all of creation in groaning for the day of full restoration (Rom. 8:18–25). One day this universe will pass away—it will be rolled up like a scroll, burned, and melted away with a roar—

and the new heavens and the new earth will descend in splendor.[6] The perfect *shalom* will be restored.

The Gatekeepers

A lot more detail can be added to these themes. But these points are critical in helping us learn to discern what we read. To discern is to authenticate something, like knowing the difference between fool's gold and 24-karat gold. The biblical worldview is like a touchstone to determine the value of gold, writes theologian Graham Cole:

> A touchstone is a piece of quartz that can be rubbed against what is claimed to be gold. The chemical reaction that follows will show whether the specimen of ore is real gold or fool's gold. The touchstone proposition acts as a gatekeeper to the house of knowledge—or so it is hoped. What we count as knowledge has to pass the quality control of the touchstone proposition. . . .
>
> There is a cluster of touchstone propositions at the heart of an intellectual account of Christianity: propositions about the Creator, the creation, the fall, the rescue, and the restoration. . . . This frame of reference not only has explanatory power—that is, it makes sense of our experience—it also raises significant questions about naturalism, secularism, modernity, postmodern relativism, naïve romanticism, utopianism, nihilism, pessimism, Islam, Hinduism, and the transhuman project as alternative stories. Frames of reference have both a positive and a negative function. They attempt to explain and to exclude.[7]

These touchstone propositions are the gatekeepers, or *control beliefs*, by which we test all other beliefs, experiences, and theories. While the Bible *does* provide us with all the divine truth we need to live a life of faith and godliness (2 Tim. 3:16), the Bible *does not* give us every truth in the universe, nor does it make that claim (it is much too short for that). No matter how much revealed truth we learn, we will always "know in part" (1 Cor. 13:9). Revealed truth does not answer all the questions in life, but it does provide a framework for understanding everything else.

This cluster of touchstone propositions is what we use to test everything else (2 Cor. 10:5). It is only on the basis of God's cohesive Word that we can ever hope to make sense of the details of information in this world. And it is only on the basis of Scripture that we can we ever hope to untangle truth from lies, good from evil, and beauty from distortion.[8]

Worldview Salad

In light of what we read in Scripture, what do we do with books that are clearly *not* written from a Christian worldview? Should we read them? Should we burn them?

First, it's important that we understand that each person's worldview is assembled from many composite details. In his book, *Meaning at the Movies: Becoming a Discerning Viewer*, Christian Grant Horner makes this point well in helping Christians evaluate worldviews on the big screen. Horner writes:

> Every worldview is the aggregate, composite result of a collection of philosophical positions—individual beliefs, presuppositions, and accepted propositions. Worldviews are made up of one or more philosophical positions working together and providing a framework for understanding the world and living in it. A worldview is like a salad; the ingredients are the various individual philosophical elements that make up the whole final flavor. All worldviews are philosophical positions, but not all individual philosophical positions are full-fledged worldviews.[9]

The worldview of an author—no matter how complementary or contradictory it appears—is informed by a collection of elements. This partly explains why at many points the Christian worldview can and will agree at times with the ingredients in a non-Christian worldview. For example, non-Christian writers can perceive the incredible dignity of humanity. Or, authors can sense something of the darkness of sin within the human heart. Often, authors can sense man's need for a "savior" of some sort. Christians can agree with these truths and even benefit from how those truths are illustrated in literature.

Non-Christian worldviews, no matter how faulty, are rarely (if ever) entirely false.[10] Non-Christians may perceive particular truths, genuine moral goodness, or aesthetic beauty. The fatal problem with a nonbiblical worldview is that the fragments of truth, goodness, and beauty that are perceived can never be assembled into a cohesive picture of God's world. The best non-Christian worldviews may include truth, but those random truths will never reveal the scope of God's saving plan.

Gene Veith explains it well:

> Humanly devised worldviews are small, partial, reducing the complexities of life into a simplistic answer. They are narrow-minded. The Christian worldview, in contrast, is whole, vast, sophisticated. . . . Since truth exists beyond ourselves and is grounded in the will and the work of God, Christians can affirm truth wherever we find it. We can build on what is of value in whatever we read. But this is only possible if we read with skepticism, refusing to accept human ideologies as authoritative, recognizing just how incomplete they are, and supplementing what they say with the larger truths found in Scripture.[11]

Scripture provides us with the only cohesive and consistent worldview. Scripture equips us to evaluate what we read in books, and helps us better perceive truth wherever it appears.

Christians can read a broad array of books for our personal benefit, but only if we read with discernment. And we will only read with discernment if the biblical convictions are firmly settled in our minds and hearts. Once they are, we have a touchstone to determine what is pure gold and what is worthless.

Reading across the Canyon

Atheist novelist Albert Camus once wrote, "A novel is never anything but a philosophy put into images."[12] Novelists animate a worldview by placing it within in a depiction of life. Literature gives a worldview arms, legs, ears, hands, and mouths. Novels activate a particular worldview.

The biblical worldview will make us keenly aware of the wide gulf of differences between ourselves, as Christian readers, and the majority of authors. Christian poet T. S. Eliot wrote, "So long as we are conscious of the gulf fixed between ourselves and the greater part of contemporary literature, we are more or less protected from being harmed by it, and are in a position to extract from it what good it has to offer us."[13] The less in common we have with an author, the greater the distance we see between us, the more discerningly we will read, and the less likely we will be duped by fool's gold.

Eliot's point helps me better appreciate literature by authors with whom I disagree overall. It also explains why the most treacherous spiritual dangers arise from theologically twisted books written by wolves in sheepskin. The greatest dangers arise when the gap is assumed to be small. Spiritual dangers are more venomous in a so-called "Christian" book. "For no heresy has ever sprung from pagan belief, from Aristotle, and from the books of other heathen," wrote Martin Luther. "No, these necessarily emerge from the church." He takes it a step further when he writes "heresy and false doctrine are taken and adduced from no other source than Scripture."[14] Luther is quick to affirm here that Scripture is pure and unadulterated in itself. But when a truth of Scripture is pulled out and warped in the hands of someone *within the church,* heresy is born. The resulting error is more dangerous than any error that originates *outside the church.* Luther's point is an important one. Heresy is dangerous because it camouflages itself as the truth, it resembles the truth, it emerges from within the church as a mistreatment of Scripture. On the other hand, books that are obviously non-Christian in orientation are far less likely to spiritually deceive us because we hold these books at a distance, we approach them with a guarded detachment, and we open the cover fully expecting to disagree with the author.

The bigger point is that by clutching tightly to a worldview that is informed by Scripture, *we* set the agenda. The author will not be allowed to lead us along blindly. We read more safely when our understanding of Scripture is sharp. As we mature here, the mist in the canyon will lift and we will better understand the gap that separates us from a majority of contemporary authors. Once we can clearly see the ravine, a large library of literature is unlocked for our benefit, and we can read from a safe distance.

Books to Avoid

So how does worldview impact my book reading decisions? Specifically, how does it inform what books I should *avoid* reading? Here are three categories that help me make this important decision.

1. Avoid Certain Books because of Timing

It is wise not to read some books because of their timing, not merely because of their content. At nine years old, my son is a voracious reader. Yet my wife and I have restricted him from reading the Harry Potter series in his private reading. We are not trying to shield him from the world. We have chosen to limit his private reading diet for the same fundamental reason that we don't send young boys into war. For a young man to develop into a warrior, he first must learn the tactics of battle and develop the muscles and instincts of a warrior. So, too, our children—and those who are children in the faith—need time to grow the deep roots of a biblical worldview before being called to exercise that worldview against the force of culture displayed in non-Christian books.

This conviction does not prevent me from reading spiritually challenging fiction books to our children verbally. In those settings I can stop and address concerns as we go along. The question here is about our child's private reading. Choosing what books to read is often not a *yes/no* decision but a *now/later* decision.

The same is true for young Christians who are new to the faith. Be cautious of reading literature that you are ill-equipped to read with discernment. Sometimes the proper Christian approach to literature is humble postponement.

2. Avoid Certain Books That Glorify Evil

I do not encourage you to avoid books that *mention* evil. Many of the greatest works in literature are written from a perspective that captures the dark realities of life. This makes it impossible to reject books merely because they include bloody violence, illicit sexuality, scornful unbelief, or dark witchcraft. The Bible includes stories of all four.

The more important questions are these: How is the violence, sexual sin, and skepticism presented? Is it presented as evil? Is fornication celebrated, or are the consequences of sin made obvious? Does the book celebrate sin, or leave evil unresolved?

Deciding what not to read is a matter of discernment, writes Peter Leithart:

> No reader, of course, has a red phone to heaven, nor is there an inerrant and infallible Index of Forbidden Books. Yet God has passed judgment on certain things, and it would be remarkable arrogance for a Christian to disagree. We know that books are bad if they pattern our desires to hope for anonymous sex, if they encourage imitation of characters who scorn God, if they invite us to see the world as a cosmic toilet.[15]

We approach all books with a discerning mind and a guarded heart. If the author intends to glorify sin and unbelief, we should not read the book, unless our goal is criticism. Scripture clearly forbids Christians from being captivated by human philosophy, by a way of thinking that is hostile to God and to his will (Col. 2:8). But Scripture does not forbid us from reading books that include descriptions of evil. We will unpack this idea in chapter 9.

3. Avoid Certain Books for Conscience's Sake

Conforming to non-Christian thought patterns is dangerous to our souls (Rom. 12:2). So how much error and sin should we endure in the name of cultural appreciation? Where is the line? Even if evil is presented, how much adultery and fornication and violence and deceit should we tolerate in our search for goodness, truth, and beauty?

This is a matter of conscience for each believer. And while there are no rigid rules for what Christians should or should not read, we must be sensitive to our own consciences and the consciences of those around us. As we establish our own understanding of what books we will and will not read ourselves, we must respect the parameters that other Christians have chosen to set for themselves and for their children.

Conclusion

Non-Christian worldviews come in many forms and under many different names. And many of these worldviews are evaluated in the book *The Universe Next Door: A Basic Worldview Catalog* by James Sire, a good resource if you want to contrast the most common worldviews in the world with a biblical worldview. A firm grasp of biblical worldview, learned directly from the study of Scripture, is essential for a Christian book reader because distortions to the biblical worldview can be found on every shelf in the bookstore.

A biblical worldview, informed by the touchstone propositions of Scripture, is what distinguishes Christian readers from non-Christian readers. It equips us to see and treasure the truth, goodness, and beauty in Christian books (the books on *our side* of the canyon). And the biblical worldview helps us see and treasure the truth, goodness, and beauty in non-Christian books (the books on *the other side* of the canyon).

5

The Giver's Voice

Seven Benefits of Reading
Non-Christian Books

What types of books should Christians read? Scripture is the most important book, and the highest priority in our reading. *Christian* books can teach us valuable lessons about God, the world, our sin, and our Savior. But in this chapter I want to focus on the value of *non-Christian* books. By that term, I mean any book not authored by a converted Christian or written from an explicitly Christian motive. What should we do with all these books? Should we burn them? Should we treasure them? Should we read them in secret under the bedsheets with a flashlight?

My conviction is that non-Christian literature—at least the best of it—is a gift from God to be read by Christians. These books are, in the words of Spurgeon, gold leaf compared to the gold bars of Scripture, but they *are* gold, and they do have value.

John Calvin
My appreciation for non-Christian books has been directly shaped by the example and writings of French Reformer John Calvin (1509–

1564). Scholars may disagree on various aspects of Calvin's theology, but few can question the prominence of three pillars in his theology (ideas reflected earlier in this book):

- No book is superior to Scripture.
- Everyone is sinful, and that sin causes spiritual blindness.
- The sinner's search for God and for ultimate truth is in vain without the gospel and the illuminating power of the Holy Spirit.

By these priorities, Calvin is qualified to help us righty determine the value of non-Christian books in the Christian life.

My first exposure to Calvin on this topic was in reading his classic theology work, *The Institutes of the Christian Religion*. At one point Calvin appraises the value of books on science, medicine, mathematics, and philosophy written by "profane authors" (by which he means thoughtful non-Christian writers, not raunchy romance novelists). Calvin writes:

> Therefore, in reading profane authors, the admirable light of truth displayed in them should remind us that the human mind, however much fallen and perverted from its original integrity, is still adorned and invested with admirable gifts from its Creator. If we reflect that the Spirit of God is the only fountain of truth, we will be careful, as we would avoid offering insult to him, not to reject or condemn truth wherever it appears. *In despising the gifts, we insult the Giver.*[1]

Calvin is saying that if we despise truth in non-Christian books, we ultimately "insult the Giver." At first those words jarred me, but I've come to see Calvin's point. God is behind all truth, even the truth that is expressed in non-Christian literature. Truth cannot be fabricated, writes Calvin.

> All truth is from God; and consequently, if wicked men have said anything that is true and just, we ought not to reject it; for it has come from God. Besides, all things are of God; and, therefore, why

66

should it not be lawful to dedicate to his glory everything that can properly be employed for such a purpose?[2]

Calvin understands what we discovered in the last chapter: a cohesive biblical worldview makes it possible for us to perceive and cherish the truth we read in non-Christian books.

For Calvin, reading non-Christian literature is like sifting Rocky Mountain streams for glittering flakes of gold. He sees a lot of river-bed silt in the pan. But those with cool patience and a keen eye will eventually discover flakes of gold. And that gold can be traced back to the vein of pure gold—God. By rejecting truth in non-Christian books, readers are rejecting God's gifts.

Let's get even more specific. I see at least seven benefits to reading (carefully selected) non-Christian books.

1. Non-Christian Literature Can Describe the World, How It Functions, and How to Subdue It

Non-Christian thinkers are graced with keen insights into the physical mechanics of our world. And Christians can benefit from non-Christian research in the areas of physical creation like science, medicine, chemistry, and mathematics. This skill to observe and to subdue the earth is a gift from the Creator given to all mankind (Gen. 1:26–31). We should study these books with care, wrote Calvin. "If the Lord has willed that we be helped in physics, dialectic, mathematics, and other like disciplines, by the work and ministry of the ungodly, let us use this assistance. For if we neglect God's gift freely offered in these arts, we ought to suffer just punishment for our sloths."[3] Scientific discovery is a gift from God that should be put to good use, no matter the author.

2. Non-Christian Books Highlight Common Life Experiences

Spiritually speaking, a wide gulf divides the redeemed from the unredeemed. Christians have been born again and have been made citizens of God's kingdom. Those who are not redeemed remain under the guilt of their sins and under the wrath of God. The distinction is quite clear. But similarities remain.

All humans share a common human experience.[4] Believers and skeptics both know what it's like to laugh at humorous stories. We both know the joy of holding a newborn child in our arms. We are both drawn to look reflectively at waves crashing along the ocean shoreline. We are saddened at the death of family and friends. We grieve over broken friendships. We have passions that motivate us. We fight side-by-side in the same wars. We are sickened by the same diseases. We are healed in the same hospitals. God blesses all of us with fruitful rains and warm sunshine (Matt. 5:45). He offers food and drink to gladden the heart and strengthen the bodies of the believer and unbeliever alike (Ps. 104:15; Acts 14:17). Morally, we both have a conscience, and in many cases we can agree on what is right and what is wrong (Rom. 2:14–16).

In this common bond of human experience, non-Christian authors have the power to connect with Christian readers through written words—to move us to awe, to tears, and to laughter. At this human level, we can read and appreciate the *human*-ness of non-Christian literature.

3. Non-Christian Books Can Expose the Human Heart

Non-Christian literature is often very honest about evil. And when that literature is thoughtful, it can provide keen insights into our fallen world.

Cormac McCarthy is one example. In his Pulitzer Prize winning novel *The Road* (2006), McCarthy ventures a guess at what would happen if the structures of human order—not to mention a majority of the earth's population—are burned away and each survivor is governed by self-interest. The result is a postapocalyptic hell. In this novel I do see a flickering flame of hope, but no Savior. From the eyes of a fiction author I see clearly the depth of sin in the human heart.

The church benefits from non-Christian literature like this in two ways.

First, books that expose sinful hearts are useful in pastoral training. Take the example of biblical counselor David Powlison, who uses "dark realism" in his seminary classes. Students are asked to read non-Christian fiction like *Death of a Salesman* by Arthur Miller,

The Iceman Cometh by Eugene O'Neill, *Heart of Darkness* by Joseph Conrad, and *The Plague* by Albert Camus. The sinful human heart is perplexing, but books like these can benefit pastors (and nonpastors) as they study the heart and seek to care for others (Jer. 17:9).

Second, books that honestly reveal sin can stir our hearts for the lost. Too often we find ourselves insulated in a Christian bubble that makes it hard to recall the despair we experienced outside of Christ. Books can explode this Christian bubble with the needlepoint of realism. So writes English professor Gene Fant:

> Reading the hopelessness of, say, Albert Camus's *The Stranger* provides a strong reminder of the hopelessness of a lost world. Such works contain the yawp and cry of a dying world that knows it is damned and seeks solace and satisfaction in things that do not provide ultimate healing. Meursault (*The Stranger's* main character) projects the voice of the dark night of the soul in which most of the world lives. His thoughts contain the dim memories of the kind of life a Christian lived before submitting to the lordship of Christ, memories which are heavy with regret and a lack of hope. The weight of Meursault's darkness of soul should move the audience to tears. If it moves Christian readers to shed the same tears for the lostness of neighbors and other fellow persons, then even Camus has provided godly thoughts to at least one reader.[5]

Non-Christian literature that deals honestly with sin and evil can be useful in the church. It can help pastors better understand the heart and it can help all Christians sympathize with the despair of those who are enslaved to sin and remain under God's wrath.

4. *Non-Christian Books Can Teach Us Wisdom and Valuable Moral Lessons*

Every culture treasures its wise sages. Even Scripture shows a level of respect toward the wise men of pagan cultures. Bible commentator Derek Kidner notes that while the Old Testament prophets are quick to curse pagan priests and magicians, the wise pagan sages are treated with much greater care and respect.[6]

You may remember that "Moses was instructed *in all the wisdom of the Egyptians*, and he was mighty in his words and deeds" (Acts 7:22). Moses's writing, thinking, and leadership skills were developed within a polytheistic culture. His pagan training provided him with an educational foundation. Likewise, Daniel was educated in "the literature and language of the Chaldeans," later becoming *superior* to all his classmates in wisdom (Dan. 1:4, 20). In the case of Moses and Daniel, it appears the pagan wisdom helped advance their personal development.

But perhaps no Old Testament character was more familiar with a wide range of Near Eastern wisdom than Solomon. Solomon's wisdom far *surpassed* that of the pagan sages. Because Solomon was so wise, his palace drew crowds of visitors and became a center of wisdom in the Ancient Near East (1 Kings 4:29–34). Perhaps Solomon only lectured, but that's doubtful. It seems Solomon listened, too.

To illustrate this point, compare Ecclesiastes 9:7–9 with a brief excerpt from the ancient pagan Babylonian literature titled *The Epic of Gilgamesh*, which was written long before Solomon was born. Note the parallels.

The Epic of Gilgamesh vs. Ecclesiastes 9:7–9

The Epic of Gilgamesh	Ecclesiastes 9:7–9
Thou, Gilgamesh, let full be thy belly, Make thou merry by day and by night. Of each day make thou a feast of rejoicing, Day and night dance thou and play! Let thy garments be sparkling fresh, Thy head be washed; bathe thou in water. Pay heed to the little one that holds on to thy hand, Let thy spouse delight in thy bosom! For this is the task of [mankind]![7]	Go, eat your bread with joy, and drink your wine with a merry heart, for God has already approved what you do. Let your garments be always white. Let not oil be lacking on your head. Enjoy life with the wife whom you love, all the days of your vain life that he has given you under the sun, because that is your portion in life and in your toil at which you toil under the sun.

It's not hard to see the parallel themes: eating and drinking, feasting, clothing, washing, and a husband rejoicing in his wife. Commentators believe that because *The Epic of Gilgamesh* is so obviously in view, the author of Ecclesiastes must have been familiar with the literature of surrounding cultures. In fact this explains why some scholars believe Solomon authored Ecclesiastes.[8]

But this is not the only place Solomon may be making select use of pagan literature. A handful of Proverbs resemble the wisdom literature of Ancient Near Eastern cultures. The writings of the ancient Egyptian sage Amenemope seem to inform what we read in Proverbs 22:17–23:11. Solomon himself makes it clear that in this section he is drawing from the wisdom of others (i.e., the "sayings of the wise"; 22:17; 24:23). Here in Proverbs it is quite likely that small portions of the ancient Egyptian wisdom were reworked and modified and incorporated into the Israelite wisdom (all under the guiding hand of the Holy Spirit). The evidence seems to indicate that this is the case.[9]

Where exactly the biblical wisdom draws from the surrounding cultural wisdom (or where the cultural wisdom draws from Israel's wisdom!) is not always clear, and research on who took what from whom can get dicey and complicated. But the general point is clear—the holy nation of Israel in the Old Testament made use of the available pagan wisdom. "The openness to learning from the wisdom of other peoples reflects the theological conviction that the God of Israel is God of all nations and of all of life," writes theologian John Goldingay. "It is not therefore surprising when other peoples perceive truths about life which the people of God can also profit from."[10]

We see other examples of this openness to learning throughout church history. Take Martin Luther's use of *Aesop's Fables*, Greek moral tales written between 620–560 BC (think the tortoise and the hare). The stories remain popular today. Luther prized the wisdom of *Aesop's Fables* and planned to translate all of *Aesop's Fables* into German—just as he had the Bible. Although he translated only fourteen of the fables, Luther said that, second to the Bible, he treasured the fables for their moral value in training children.[11]

Of course the wisdom of Amenemope and Aesop, like the wisdom we can find in many contemporary books written by non-

Christians, will not save you. It cannot give you spiritual life. It is not the gospel.

But that does not permit us to close our ears. There is wisdom in non-Christian books that is consistent with Scripture and *useful* for wise living. Throughout history Christians have appreciated portions of non-Christian wisdom, not because Christians have a high view of human authors, but because they have an exalted appreciation for the Giver who is the source of all moral goodness, even the moral goodness perceived in the conscience of a pagan writer (Rom. 2:14–16).[12]

5. Non-Christian Books Can Capture Beauty

In the Bible, *beauty* is presented as "a general artistic quality denoting the positive response of a person to nature, a person or an artifact."[13] Beauty is not easy to define, but it's hard to miss. Men can be beautiful. Women can be beautiful, too, especially internally (1 Pet. 3:3–4). And children can be beautiful. Michelangelo captures external physical beauty in marble statues.

Beauty, like anything, can be deformed by sin. But fundamentally, *all beauty finds its origin in the Creator* (Gen. 1:31; Eccles. 3:11). The beauty of the human body, a statue, a painting, a song, or a novel is all God-given. He gives us this beauty to enjoy, and that includes beautifully written books by non-Christians.

"Literature and art are God's gifts to the human race," writes literature scholar Leland Ryken. "One of the liberating effects of letting ourselves 'go' as we enjoy literature is to realize that we can partly affirm the value of literature whose content or worldview we dislike. If God is the ultimate source of all beauty and artistry, then the artistic dimension of literature is the point at which Christians can be unreserved in their enthusiasm for the works of non-Christian writers."[14] This point is critical for book readers. Our freedom to enjoy the aesthetic beauty of non-Christian literature does not require us to first endorse the author's worldview or personal ethical choices.

The ability to enjoy artistic beauty without embracing the author's worldview, and without affirming the moral integrity of the artist, is something God himself can do, according to theologian Richard Mouw: "When an unbelieving poet makes use of an apt metaphor we can think of God as enjoying the event without necessarily approving of anything in the agents involved."[15] God is reflected in all truth, goodness, and beauty of this world. It is reasonable to think that God delights in all those reflections of himself without necessarily approving of the spiritual condition of the sinner. Likewise, Christian readers can enjoy the beauty in the literature of non-Christian authors because that literature images the beauty of God, regardless of the personal moral and spiritual condition of the author.

God is the source of all beauty, and beautiful literature written by non-Christians is a gift from the Giver. And it's a gift to be enjoyed.

6. Non-Christian Literature Begs Questions That Can Only Be Resolved in Christ

Paul's address to a pagan audience in Acts 17:16–34 provides a compelling biblical example of the value of non-Christian literature as a bridge between contemporary culture and the gospel. Here Paul quotes directly from two pagan poets (v. 28). The Greek poet Epimenides provides the first: "In him we live and move and have our being." Stoic poet Aratus provides the second quote: "For we are indeed his offspring." It appears both excerpts are taken from pagan poems written to exalt Zeus.[16]

Clearly Paul was familiar with the pagan literature of his day and did not find it necessary to denounce it—at least not here. This is a little surprising, given the disturbing abundance of cultural idols (v. 16). Yet in both instances, Paul uses the poetic excerpts constructively, finding in them an echo of spiritual truth about God and about the nature of our relationship to him as our Creator.[17]

Here in Acts 17, Paul acknowledges the Greco-Roman impulse to seek after God. He enters the idol-saturated city of Athens to encourage the people to seek God in the gospel of Jesus Christ. "What therefore you worship as unknown, this I proclaim to you" (v. 23).

Ultimately what the pantheistic poets sought in Zeus and other deities is found only in the living God and in Jesus Christ. In many ways these spiritual impulses were legit. But these spiritual impulses were also futile. Unsubmitted to the gospel, all searches for God are ultimately choked out by sin, the truth about God that is revealed in creation is suppressed, and the impulse to worship is expressed in the vain worship of gold, silver, and stone idols (v. 29; see also Rom. 1:18–32).

Yet there remains in the pagans a pursuit of religion and a genuine spiritual impulse to worship. Theologian Herman Bavinck explains:

> All the elements and forms that are essential to religion (a concept of God, a sense of guilt, a desire for redemption, sacrifice, priesthood, temple, cult, prayer, etc.), though corrupted, nevertheless do also occur in pagan religions. . . . Hence Christianity is not only positioned antithetically toward paganism; it is also paganism's fulfillment. Christianity is the true religion, therefore also the highest and purest; it is the truth of all religions. What in paganism is the caricature, the living original is here. What is appearance there is essence here. What is sought there can be found here.[18]

Paul perceived these "elements and forms" in the pagan literature in his own day. This explains why he opposed the idolatry of paganism and at the same time valued what was true in the pagan poets. He comprehended these "elements and forms" in the poets, in light of their ultimate and final fulfillment in Christ.

Paul illustrates this point elsewhere. He found that his Jewish listeners demanded from him a powerful display of signs and wonders. His Greek listeners demanded from him profoundly articulated wisdom. Paul offers them power *and* wisdom in the crucified Messiah (although in a much different form than his audiences expected!). For Paul, "Christ crucified" is the ultimate display of power and wisdom. We discover the power of God in the weakness of the cross. We discover the wisdom of God in the foolishness of the cross. Incredibly, the human desires for spiritual power and wisdom find in the gospel both their antithesis and their ultimate expression (1 Cor. 1:22–25).

In many respects the non-Christian literature we read today is different from what Paul quotes in Acts 17, but I think his general approach is still useful for book readers. His approach will protect us from posturing ourselves *only* antithetically to the religious impulses of our culture. And from that posture we can discover that non-Christian authors occasionally articulate genuine spiritual desires that we know can be satisfied nowhere else but in the living original, in the essence, in Christ himself.

7. Non-Christian Books Can Echo Spiritual Truth and Edify the Soul

Basil of Caesarea (ca. AD 330–379) and Augustine of Hippo (AD 354–430) are two early church fathers that shaped John Calvin's appreciation for non-Christian books. In a lecture to help young Christian men navigate the flood of Greek literature, Basil said, "Heathen learning is not unprofitable for the soul." Later he encouraged the young men that, "For the journey of this life eternal I would advise you to husband resources, leaving no stone unturned, as the proverb has it, whence you might derive any aid."[19]

Similarly, Augustine encouraged Christian readers to intellectually plunder the pages of pagan literature. Augustine believed that "if those who are called philosophers, and especially the Platonists, have said aught that is true and in harmony with our faith, we are not only not to shrink from it, but to claim it for our own use."[20] He continues:

All branches of heathen learning have not only false and superstitious fancies and heavy burdens of unnecessary toil, which every one of us, when going out under the leadership of Christ from the fellowship of the heathen, ought to abhor and avoid; but they contain also liberal instruction which is better adapted to the use of the truth, and some most excellent precepts of morality; and some truths in regard even to the worship of the One God are found among them.[21]

Augustine invited Christian readers to borrow richly from the "gold leaf" found in non-Christian literature to illustrate matters of theology, ethics, and even worship. Augustine was not attempting to force pagan philosophy into the church. And he was certainly not a syncretist trying to reconcile Scripture with paganism. Augustine used Scripture as his guide to discern what was true and false in non-

Christian books.[22] The truth originated in God. And for Augustine, whatever was true was useful.

Calvin carried on this tradition. For example, while teaching on the Lord's Prayer, Calvin quotes this pagan prayer from the works of Plato (427–347 BC):

> King Jupiter, bestow the best things upon us whether we wish for them or not, but command that evil things be far from us even when we request them.[23]

King Jupiter, the thunderbolt-firing Roman god of destiny? We are right to question why Calvin is quoting this prayer. How can this prayer instruct Christians in the spiritual disciplines?

In Plato's prayer, Calvin made an edifying discovery. Plato laments that his own prayers to the mythical god Jupiter were ironically self-defeating. Upon reading the pagan prayer, Calvin recognized that it supported an important biblical truth. Said Calvin,

> The heathen man is wise in that he judges how dangerous it is to seek from the Lord what our greed dictates; at the same time he discloses our unhappiness, in that we cannot even open our mouths before God without danger unless the Spirit instructs us in the right pattern for prayer [Rom. 8:26].[24]

The pagan prayer was instructive, and Calvin felt the freedom to use it to instruct Christians. Like Plato we often pray for things that would destroy us, if we got them. Plato teaches the Christian to depend upon the Holy Spirit even in our requests.

When necessary, Calvin roasted Plato for his errors and for his overall theological blindness.[25] But where Plato was right, Plato was useful. And where Plato was useful, Calvin was free to benefit from his teaching and to use that teaching to illustrate biblical truth.[26]

Contemporary literature echoes biblical truth, too. John Piper once wrote "there are pointers to Christ in every philosophy."[27] He wrote that phrase in an article voicing his public appreciation (and criticism) for the philosophy of atheist Ayn Rand and her novel *Atlas Shrugged* (1957). Despite Rand's commitment to atheism, *Atlas*

Shrugged reflects a pursuit of pleasure that looks similar to what Piper reads in Scripture. It is, in his language, "so close and yet so far to what I find in the Bible."[28] And that's a fitting phrase.

In non-Christian works we discover what is so close, and yet so far away, from what we read in the Bible. The challenge is to make use of the "so close" for our edification and for the glory of God while being aware of the "yet so far away."

Sweet Corn

As book readers, we are mistaken when we categorically reject non-Christian books. And we are mistaken when we read non-Christian literature uncritically. Calvin avoided both blunders. Calvin read non-Christian literature with caution, yet he always postured himself to experience "splendid encounters" with the Giver of all truth, goodness, and beauty.[29] Cornelius Plantinga sums up Calvin's approach to non-Christian literature well:

> Calvin understood that God created human beings to hunt and gather truth, and that, as a matter of fact, the capacity for doing so amounts to one feature of the image of God in them (Col. 3:10). So Calvin fed on knowledge as gladly as a deer on sweet corn. He absorbed not only the teaching of Scripture and of its great interpreters, such as St. Augustine, but also whatever knowledge he could gather from such famous pagans as the Roman philosopher Seneca. And why not? The Holy Spirit authors all truth, as Calvin wrote, and we should therefore embrace it no matter where it shows up. But we will need solid instruction in Scripture and Christian wisdom in order to recognize truth and in order to disentangle it from error and fraud. Well-instructed Christians try not to offend the Holy Spirit by scorning truth in non-Christian authors over whom the Spirit has been brooding, but this does not mean that Christians can afford to read these authors uncritically. After all, a person's faith, even in idols, shapes most of what a person thinks and writes, and the Christian faith is in competition with other faiths for human hearts and minds.[30]

I find Calvin's model *generous*, *cautious*, and *sobering*.

Calvin's model is *generous,* because it humbly acknowledges the wealth of truth, goodness, and beauty articulated in non-Christian literature. Sinners do suppress God's truth in their behavior (Rom. 1:18–32). But it is impossible for sinners to suppress *all* the truth *all* the time.[31] The truth, goodness, and wisdom that glows in the writings of non-Christian books is truth, goodness, and wisdom that finds its ultimate origin in the Creator. Calvin sought to humbly recognize and receive these gifts wherever they could be found, and to thank God for them.

Calvin's model is also *cautious.* Non-Christian authors are spiritually blind. Any light of truth in their writings is powerless to lead them to Christ and to salvation. Only the Holy Spirit can open the blind eyes of a sinner to see the blazing glory of the Savior.

Calvin's model is also *sobering* because it reminds us that the truth gleaned by non-Christian authors only increases his or her sinful guilt. Truth discovered in non-Christian literature may glow brightly in our eyes, but for authors not washed in Christ's blood, these truths bear a heavier guilt upon their souls before God and reveal their damnable lack of obedience and lack of gratitude to God (Rom. 1:21).

Conclusion

As Basil would say in his lecture to young men on the proper use of Greek poetry, "The soul must be guarded with great care, lest through our love for letters [reading] it receive some contamination unawares, as men drink in poison with honey."[32] Amen. We must be careful.

The goal of this chapter is *not* to persuade you to fill up your library and your reading diet with non-Christian novels, the latest pop-spiritual writings, or the hippest new philosophy. In fact, this would be unwise. And until you have a functional biblical worldview (which may require a number of years), it may be wise for you to stay away from a majority of non-Christian books. At least for a time.

The bottom line is that I cannot reject non-Christian literature, nor give wholesale approval to it. This is an unresolved tension for the Christian reader. The Christian reader must simply treasure whatever is true, honorable, just, pure, lovely, commendable, excellent, or praiseworthy (Phil. 4:8)—wherever it is found. If a Christian reader is attuned to the whisper of the Giver, he will hear that whisper in some very unexpected places.

6

The God Who Slays Dragons

The Purifying Power of Christian Imagination

To *imagine* is to picture things in your head. It is the ability to "see" things in your mind that you cannot immediately see with your eyes.

Let me flex your imagination with two little experiments.

Here is imagination exercise 1: Imagine in your mind that it's a hot summer night. You decide to do a mundane chore: gather the garbage from inside your house and drop it in the trash can outside. You grab a large garbage bag and work from room to room, loading the trash. When the bag is full, you cinch the top and carry it outside. As you approach the can and lift the lid, you gag on the noxious smell of warmed garbage. You hold your breath, turn your head, drop the garbage bag, close the lid, and gasp for fresh air as you head back inside.

Now stop and rewind the situation. Here is a little different take.

Imagination exercise 2: Imagine that you walk outside with your bag of garbage. You lift the trash can lid. But this time as you lift the lid, a stunning thing happens: like it was trapped there against its will, an arc of sapphire blue light, rockets out of the can, rainbows over the neighbor's house, and lands somewhere three miles away.

Startled and blinded, you drop the bag of garbage in the grass. The darkness returns, and you throw the lid back down on the can. Your eyes readjust to the night, and you look around to see if the neighbors noticed the scene. You walk back inside and close the door, stunned and speechless.

These illustrations stink. I know. But they illustrate an important lesson, because while both stories require your imagination, they require two distinct uses of the imagination: *primary* and *secondary*.

In example 1 we engage our *primary imagination*. Our minds can picture the scene because our minds recall what we have already seen and experienced. We've all seen a trash can. Even worse, we know what a trash can smells like on a warm summer night (especially if you, like me, have kids in diapers!).

In example 2 we engage our *secondary imagination*. This is a situation that I have never experienced, and I doubt you have either. Yet did you find the shooting light in example 2 more difficult to imagine than the scene in example 1? Likely not. God has given us the ability to "see" in our minds things that we have never experienced.

The primary sense of imagination (seeing in our minds what we've seen before) is a skill that we probably share with other creatures. The secondary sense of imagination (seeing in our minds what we've never experienced) is a distinctly human skill. Some might say it's a *spiritual* skill.[1] God has given us this higher use of imagination to enable us to create art, make scientific discoveries, further technological progress, and write poetry. And God has given us an imagination so that our book reading will be more effective.

In this chapter I argue that our secondary imagination is essential for our pursuit of godliness, and that it's a skill we can sharpen by reading. But first I want to ask: Where does our imagination come from?

God's Imagination

We imagine because God imagines. In fact, before the world began, everything merely existed in God's imagination. Entire chapters could be devoted to God's imaginative genius on display in creation:

the design of the sun, planets, plants, animals, molecules, DNA, and more.

But God's imaginative genius is also displayed in the gospel. Think about it. The gospel weaves together a genealogy of dodgy characters into an unlikely ancestry for the Savior. The gospel was foretold by centuries of ancient prophecies, many of them fragmented and scattered throughout the Old Testament, to a people who could not make sense of it all. In time, the genealogy and the prophecies merged together into a cohesive plan that led to the birth of the incarnate Son of God.

So ingenious is the gospel plan, that when men and Satan conspired to kill and bury the Savior, they only hastened the Father's plan for his Son's victory. This entire plan developed in God's imagination long before the world existed (Eph. 3:7–10; 1 Pet. 1:18–20).

We imagine because our Creator imagines. And with our imagination we can now "see" eternal reality (2 Cor. 4:18). This divine imagination, this ability to see the unseen, is a skill God has given us for our spiritual profit.

Without an active imagination, a good bit of the Bible will be hard to read, difficult to understand, and impossible to appreciate. Let me show you how this works by turning to the book of Revelation.

Seven-Eyed Savior

No book in the Bible demands more from our imagination than the book of Revelation.

Just consider the symbolism found in Revelation 4. The apostle John leads us into the throne room of God. This is the "situation room," the control center where cosmic decisions are made. God is enthroned and encircled by his colonels and generals. Four living creatures join a gathering of powerful angels and twenty-four elders.

Seven flaming torches have been lit, and a crystal floor, like a silent sea, surrounds the throne of God. Lightning flashes out like Sinai, and thunder rumbles like an earthquake (4:5).

All eyes focus on an unopened scroll, sealed seven times over. This scroll contains the final chapters of God's fallen creation and the inauguration of the new heavens and the new earth. As the scroll is unrolled, the events in those chapters will unfold in real time.

"Who is worthy to open the seal?" cries an angel. Then silence. The scroll is untouched. The angels look at the elders, the elders look at the angels, and it becomes obvious that no one is worthy to open the scrolls. Will the evil in the world continue on unabated? Who will stop sin, rebellion, injustice, and chaos? Who will put an end to Satan? Who will restore creation back to the way it's supposed to be? Who will bring to fulfillment all the promises of the new heavens and the new earth?

With no one in sight and with no apparent resolution, the apostle John breaks down and weeps loudly. As tears stream down his face, an elder approaches John, and the magnificent scene unfolds:

> And one of the elders said to me, "Weep no more; behold, the Lion of the tribe of Judah, the Root of David, has conquered, so that he can open the scroll and its seven seals."
>
> And between the throne and the four living creatures and among the elders I saw a Lamb standing, as though it had been slain, with seven horns and with seven eyes, which are the seven spirits of God sent out into all the earth. And he went and took the scroll from the right hand of him who was seated on the throne. And when he had taken the scroll, the four living creatures and the twenty-four elders fell down before the Lamb, each holding a harp, and golden bowls full of incense, which are the prayers of the saints. And they sang a new song, saying,
>
> "Worthy are you to take the scroll
>   and to open its seals,
> for you were slain, and by your blood you ransomed people for God
>   from every tribe and language and people and nation,
> and you have made them a kingdom and priests to our God,
>   and they shall reign on the earth." (Rev. 5:5–10)

The obvious centerpiece of this chapter—the centerpiece of heaven!—is the Lamb of God who was slain to ransom sinners. Universal attention is focused on the seven-eyed, seven-horned, slain-looking Lamb.

When we imagine a conquering king, we think of a jaw-clenched Caesar with a silver sword, not a conquering Lamb with lethal wounds. In their attempt to capture this image in the painting *Adoration of the Lamb* (1432), Hubert and Jan van Eyck picture a white lamb, surefooted and balanced, with crimson blood spurting from a wound in its chest. It's a noble attempt, but no painting can capture all the details of this scene.

So what's the point of Revelation's image of our Savior here? The seven eyes represent that Jesus is *all-seeing*; nothing is hidden from his view. The seven horns mean Jesus is *all-powerful*; nothing escapes his rule. And although he gave his life to be slain, his wounds are the marks of a conqueror who was killed while defeating an enemy.[2]

The point of the images is straightforward: Jesus is worthy of all our praise!

But instead of merely saying *Jesus is worthy*, God engages the eye of our imagination to *see* just how worthy the seven-eyed and seven-horned Lamb really is. The image stuns us in a way that a simple declaration cannot.

The God Who Slays Dragons

A second example of symbolism is found in another pivotal chapter in Revelation (12:1–6).

Again, the story is clothed in the language of fantasy, but the point is absolutely true. The story features a pregnant woman, a child, and a very nasty predator—a red, bloodthirsty dragon. It's a different version of the Christmas story than we will put on our holiday cards this year.

The red dragon in the story is Satan; the pregnant woman here is not Mary, but rather an embodiment of the Messianic community, the community of believers; the woman's unborn child is the Messiah. The story picks up as the woman prepares to give birth to her child (the Messiah).

The dragon swoops in for the kill.

The shocking labor and delivery room scene looks like this, writes D. A. Carson:

The scene is grotesque. The dragon stands in front of the woman. She is lying there in labor. Her feet are in the stirrups, writhing as she pushes to give birth, and this disgusting dragon is waiting to grab the baby as it comes out of the birth canal and then eat it (12:4). The scene is meant to be grotesque: it reflects the implacable rage of Satan against the arriving Messiah.[3]

Now there is a simpler and more direct way to say that Herod tried to kill baby Jesus (see Matt. 2:16). But Herod is not the point, and Herod is not the problem. The point is that behind the mask of Herod's jealousy is Satan's vicious hatred of Christ.

The story in chapter 12 is not here to entertain our curiosity. For all its imaginative elements, the story unmasks why the church is persecuted in this world. Behind the angry hate from government officials toward the Messiah, and behind the vented hostility of sinners toward the church, runs a satanic undercurrent. Throughout Scripture, the dragon symbolizes the evil forces and kingdoms that seek to destroy God's people.

Through the book of Revelation God wants us to "see" with the eyes of our imagination the deeper and unseen powers at work. Dragons function nicely for the task.

Dragons are devilish, curling, slithering beasts with wings, sometimes with flame-shooters and sometimes with multiple heads. Because the dragon is the king of all the fiercest beasts, it makes for stunning imagery. In Ezekiel 32, the Egyptian empire is pictured as a dragon churning the waters. God throws his net over the dragon, raises him to the sky, throws him down against the jagged mountains, and splits the dragon's flesh across the landscape. Rivers of blood wash down through the ravines. The birds of the air fill themselves on the conquered flesh. To display God's defeat of evil powers, fictional dragons are a perfect choice.

By using fantasy and engaging our imagination, God can reveal forces, communities, and struggles in a way that straightforward language cannot.

The Organ of Meaning

Reading and appreciating the images in Revelation requires a special skill, one I did not develop for many years as a Christian. Appreciating these biblical images is similar to appreciating impressionist paintings. Focusing on a single detail in apocalyptic literature is like studying a single brushstroke in a Claude Monet painting. The strokes only make sense when viewed as a whole. The same is true with the parts of Scripture that use fantasy to make a point. We absorb a scene, like the one in Revelation 5, by stepping back and watching the scene unfold—much like we absorb an impressionist painting.[4] Our imagination assembles the pieces into a stunning whole.

The imagination gives us the "power of synoptic vision," writes theologian Kevin Vanhoozer. It assembles pieces into a comprehensive picture and "allows us to see as whole what those who lack imagination see only as unrelated parts."[5] Through our imaginations, God connects what may otherwise seem to be scattered and disconnected events: Satan's fall, the Messiah's birth, Herod's rage, the church's persecution, and the ultimate dragon slaying in Christ's triumphant death (see Rev. 12:11). Our imagination allows us to absorb these realities together.

The imagination is a God-given ability to receive truth and meaning. In an essay, C. S. Lewis wrote, "For me *reason* is the natural organ of truth; but *imagination* is the organ of meaning."[6] Using fantasy in literature does not make a story fictitious; it's often a more forceful way to communicate truth.

But again we ask, why does God use this type of fantasy writing in the Bible? And how does this imaginative writing shape what books we choose to read?

Just Heed It

We can often decode the purpose of a book in the Bible by locating similarities and parallels at the beginning and the end of the book. This is true with Revelation. God extends his blessing to readers who *hear* his words and *heed* them. We see this at the beginning and at the end of the book (see vv. 1:3 and 22:7). Those purpose statements—*hear* and *heed*—are intended to motivate us to read Revelation.

On one hand we are blessed to *hear*. We are blessed to pay attention, blessed to read soberly and carefully, blessed to engage our imaginations and to absorb the spectacular scenes. This makes sense.

But God expects readers to *heed* the imagery. And here is where I get tripped up. Heed what? What exactly are the application points for a seven-eyed and seven-horned Jesus? What is the application point for a bloodthirsty red dragon? What are the application points for other images in Revelation—like a demonic leviathan rising from the sea with ten horns, seven heads, the mouth of a lion, the feet of a bear, and a raw, fatal wound (13:1–10)? Or how do I apply the image of Jesus with a sickle, cutting down the wicked and gathering them like grapes for the winepress of God's wrath (14:14–16)? What relation do these images have with my struggle against sin, my love for the lost, or my role as a father?

Defibrillation by Imagination

The imagery in Revelation was written to make us holy.

Greg Beale, a leading scholar on the book of Revelation, explains how. "When we begin to resemble the idols of the world, and spiritual harm is set in motion," he says, "we need pictures to shock us out of this paralysis."[7] And here is the key to understanding the purpose of the images in Revelation.

The imagination-stretching images are God's way of sliding the spiritual defibrillator over the slowing hearts of sluggish Christians. The images are for Christians who are growing lazy and beginning to compromise with the world, Christians who are allowing their hearts to become gradually hardened by sin. The answer is a spiritual shock. It is God's way of confronting worldliness and idolatry in the church. When idolatry begins to lure the Christian heart, God reaches into our imagination with images intended to stun us back to spiritual vibrancy.

This explains how the images in Revelation are *heeded*. The images give us eternal focus and cause us to reevaluate our priorities. The images fuel our zeal to kill personal sin, keep us alert to the purity of the local church, inform our counsel for fellow sinners, deepen our love for the lost, make us diligent in prayer, disgust us with personal idolatry, dissatisfy us with worldliness, and stir a longing in our hearts for Christ's return.

Revelation invites us to see ultimate reality through our imaginations, in breathtaking, earth-scorching, mind-stretching, sin-defeating, dragon-slaying, Christ-centered, God-glorifying images that change the way we think, act, and speak.

To view imaginative literature as a genre fit only for the amusement of children is an act of spiritual negligence.

The Imaginative Appetite

Much of this book is autobiographical, reflecting my journey in literature. This chapter included. In the past I avoided imaginative literature in my reading diet, favoring propositional books of straightforward principles. For years I neglected cultivating my imagination.

Once I began developing an appreciation for fantasy and imaginative literature like Homer's *The Iliad* and *The Odyssey*, C. S. Lewis's series The Chronicles of Narnia, and of course J. R. R. Tolkien's The Lord of the Rings, I discovered that my appreciation for Revelation has grown and the weight of its images have pressed heavier on my soul. As I have read imaginative literature, my imagination has developed. As my imagination has developed, I have found myself reading Revelation more patiently, allowing the images to emerge in my mind until I feel the full spiritual shock of their intended voltage.

The lesson I have learned is that a failure to cultivate the imagination leads to an unintended neglect of the imaginative literature of Scripture, and this in turn leads to some degree of spiritual atrophy. For Christians, the stories of Revelation are not optional reading. Nor are they child's play. Imaginative literature—the kind of literature that invites us to see in our imaginations what we cannot see with our eyes—is an important part of the Christian's literary diet. It challenges our idols. It challenges what is false and trivial in our lives.

PART 2

Some Practical Advice on Book Reading

7

Read with Resolve

Six Priorities That Decide What Books I Read (and Don't Read)

At last, we arrive at the application. The first six chapters set out the essential convictions that Christians need to read books well. From here, we focus more on the practical side of reading, considering a lot of tips, tricks, and how-tos.

Likely you picked up this book because you want to read more books, an excellent goal. So let's visualize this.

Imagine that you make the wildly ambitious goal of reading one book per week for the next fifty years. Lofty aspiration! If you remain faithful to the task, you will read about 2,600 books. Not bad for five decades of reading.

Now consider how many more books are available for you to read. In 2010, the minds at Google Books calculated that in human history 129,864,880 different books have been published in various languages. But I can only read in English, so let's whittle this number down a bit.

Currently, the Library of Congress houses eighteen million books. American publishers add another two hundred thousand titles to this stack each year. This means that at the current publishing rate, ten million new books will be added in the next fifty years. Add together the dusty LOC volumes with the shiny new and forthcoming books, and you get a bookshelf-warping total of twenty-eight million books available for an English reader in the next fifty years! But you can read only 2,600—because you are a wildly ambitious book devourer.

These numbers are not scientific, of course. But here is my point: For every *one* book that you choose to read, you must ignore *ten thousand* other books simply because you don't have the time (or money!). Book reading will make you acutely aware of your personal limitations.

So how do we decide what *one* book to read? Or maybe more importantly, how do we determine which *ten thousand* books to reject?

As with most areas of life, success requires planning. Having a clear purpose for why you read will ensure that the few books you choose will be the books most likely to benefit your life.

And that brings us to the task of determining our personal reading priorities.

Reading Scripture

In the first chapter, we discovered that no book is more important than the Bible. It is the divine and inspired word of God, true and reliable in everything it affirms. In it we learn the touchstone truths that shape our worldview. If we neglect Scripture in order to read only other books, we not only cut ourselves from the divine umbilical cord that feeds our souls, we also cut ourselves from the truth that makes it possible for us to benefit from the truth, goodness, and beauty in the books that we read.

So the Bible is rightly affirmed as the highest reading priority in the life of every Christian. We read the Bible to know the heart of our God, to understand better the work of our Savior, to find spiritual food for our souls, and to discover God's wisdom for our lives. Scripture is delightful, too, sweet to the soul and more valuable than gold (Pss. 19:10; 119:103).

To delight in Scripture, I read the Bible from two angles: for its details, and for its big-picture storyline.

Sometimes I want to delight in the Bible slowly and methodically, studying and comprehending one verse at a time. I use my *ESV Study Bible* for this. The study notes are helpful when the text gets thick and complicated. When I read for detail, I want Bible teachers on hand to help with questions as they arise.

Sometimes I want to delight in the Bible swiftly and broadly, reading multiple chapters in one setting. I use my *Literary Study Bible: ESV* edited by Leland Ryken and Philip Ryken for this. The chapter-by-chapter notes give me just enough preparation so that I can read swiftly across chapters of the Bible without losing sight of the storyline or slowing down for details.

The bottom line is that no single book should receive more attention in our lives than Scripture. The Bible is the greatest book and our highest priority—it ignites us with spiritual light and life, it fuels us with eternal hope and grace, and it stokes us with inexhaustible pleasure and delight.

Reading Everything Else

This chapter is an overview of all the types of books I read. Where do theology books, business books, biographies, poems, and novels fit into my reading diet?

In order to explain, I must get personal and explain how I do it. Your reading priorities will look different, maybe very different. As I explain my reading priorities, I encourage you to pull down a notebook and write out your own goals and reading priorities.

Once I have prioritized my direct study of God's Word, the rest of my reading follows. I structure my reading along these priorities:

1. Reading Scripture
2. Reading to know and delight in Christ
3. Reading to kindle spiritual reflection
4. Reading to initiate personal change
5. Reading to pursue vocational excellence
6. Reading to enjoy a good story

Allow me to explain the other five.

Reading to Know and Delight in Christ

The largest topical section in my personal library features books on the person and work of Christ. This is my second highest ranked priority, just after my direct reading of Scripture.

Christ is the centerpiece of Scripture, the focus of heaven, and the stage that displays God's glory. "For in the cross of Christ, as in a magnificent theatre, the inestimable goodness of God is displayed before the whole world," John Calvin wrote. "In all the creatures, indeed, both high and low, the glory of God shines, but nowhere has it shone more brightly than in the cross."[1]

The surpassing love of Jesus Christ is the center of my attention, and the core around which my life, my learning, and my library is built (Eph. 3:14–19).

"Almost all men are infected with the disease of desiring to obtain useless knowledge," Calvin writes. "It is of great importance that we should be told what is necessary for us to know, and what the Lord desires us to contemplate, above and below, on the right hand and on the left, before and behind. The love of Christ is held out to us as the subject which ought to occupy our daily and nightly meditations, and in which we ought to be wholly plunged."[2]

I regularly plunge my soul in solid theology books about the person and work of Christ.[3] I bathe my mind in the theological works of a few dead theologians—Calvin, Martin Luther, Jonathan Edwards, John Owen, Thomas Goodwin, Herman Bavinck, and Geerhardus Vos. And I immerse my soul into the works of contemporary authors like J. I. Packer, D. A. Carson, John Stott, R. C. Sproul, John Piper, Jerry Bridges, and C. J. Mahaney. Old or new, I prize any books that will help me swim deeply into the person, work, and love of Christ.

Theologically weighty books about Christ are essential for the soul—for men and women. And although women purchase the majority of books released by Christian publishers, women are far less likely to read theological books, writes counselor and author Elyse Fitzpatrick. In her 2003 evaluation of the Christian publishing industry, she writes, "Many women are intimidated by the thought of studying something that is 'theological' in nature. They are afraid of being bored, looking foolish, becoming unattractive to men, or becoming divisive."[4] And she confronts women who would rather read only novels as a way to escape personal disappointments, and who read these books to "build fantasy castles filled with knights on white steeds who will come to rescue her from her mundane, stressful, empty, or disappointing life." Rather, she offers this challenge: "Let's become known as a generation of women who delight in, tremble before, receive counsel from, drink, devour, digest, muse upon, and absolutely cherish God and the truth that He's revealed about Himself and about ourselves. Let's not worry about whether we look dumb or too smart."[5]

If women commit to reading books of solid theology, their knowledge of Christ will grow, because "theology (of the right sort) is about knowing God and His Son intimately. Knowledge of Him (not just about Him) feeds, transforms, and vivifies the soul. This is the most delightful pursuit any woman could ever know."

Reading to know and delight in Christ is an essential pursuit by women and men alike.

Reading to Kindle Spiritual Reflection

Perceptive readers will notice that contemporary Christian publishers often favor pragmatic books. Walk into any Christian bookstore and you will notice that "how-to" books get a lot of attention. There is a place for reading application, as we will soon see. Yet much of the Christian life is about training the mind, kindling the affections, and learning the vocabulary of the faith (1 Cor. 14:20; Rom. 12:2). This requires deep spiritual reflection on topics like faith, grace, sin, death, and eternal life.

The Christian literature that fuels my spiritual reflection comes in a variety of sizes, formats, and genres.

Fiction is one of them. I keep on hand a storehouse of able Christian novelists like C. S. Lewis, Flannery O'Connor, Marilynne Robinson, and Walter Wangerin. Good Christian novelists connect grace to life and make spiritual reflection unavoidable.

Take for example Robinson's Pulitzer-winning novel *Gilead*. Statements that foster spiritual reflection are scattered throughout her book. At one point she writes about eternity, and what role this present life will play in the life to come:

> I can't believe that, when we have all been changed and put on incorruptibility, we will forget our fantastic condition of mortality and impermanence, the great bright dream of procreating and perishing that meant the whole world to us. In eternity this world will be Troy, I believe, and all that has passed here will be the epic of the universe, the ballad they sing in the streets. Because I don't imagine any reality putting this one in the shade entirely, and I think piety forbids me to try.[6]

Reflective statements like this one are common in Robinson's novels. This excerpt makes me stop and meditate on the eternal significance of this life.

Russian novelist Fyodor Dostoevsky is another example. Dostoyevsky was a realist who sought to honestly look into the shadows of our sinful world. Within this darkness he lit the candle of grace. Unfortunately, his works can be exhaustingly long, but the patient reader will find rich material for spiritual reflection.

But perhaps no Christian author is better at using myth and fantasy for the purpose of stimulating spiritual reflection than C. S. Lewis. His seven-book The Chronicles of Narnia series is a must-read for children and adults alike. The series is filled with allegorical pictures of our Savior and his sacrifice, and the human struggle with sin and temptation. Much of the theological symbolism sits on the surface of the books.

Christian biographies and autobiographies are another great source of spiritual reflection. *The Confessions* by Augustine is a classic example. Augustine reflects honestly about life and the gospel, seamlessly weaving the language of the Psalms into the fabric of his own personal experience.

I find that spiritual reflection is kindled by great poems, too. The church has been blessed with many gifted poets, yet most of them are neglected today. I think John Donne is the supreme example. His *Holy Sonnets* are rich, powerful, and spiritually provoking. I study and reflect on these poems frequently. Here are four famous lines from a sonnet from a man who yearns for God to liberate his affections from the power of sin:

> Batter my heart, three person'd God; for you
> As yet, but knock, breathe, shine, and seek to mend,
> That I may rise and stand, overthrow me, and bend
> Your force to break, blow, burn, and make me new.[7]

In these lines we can hear the sound of the hammer smacking, smacking, smacking against the anvil as the blacksmith (the triune God) breaks and reshapes the metal (us). The famous sonnet continues for another ten lines. It paints a picture of sin's power to shackle our hearts and our need for God's grace to redeem our lives. One author summarizes this short sonnet this way: "The triune God must batter our hearts—He must break us to pieces and make us new; He must crash through the gates of our hearts; He must steal us away from Satan."[8] The poem is breathtaking.

Like no other genre, poetry can quickly stir our hearts to spiritual reflection, so it's no surprise that God included so much poetry in the Bible. Along with King David, some of my favorite poets in church history include John Donne, George Herbert, Anne Bradstreet, T. S. Eliot, Isaac Watts, and Geoffrey Chaucer. I keep a compilation of the best Christian poetry, *A Sacrifice of Praise* (edited by James Trott), on my nightstand.

So I read books to be spiritually stirred. For me this happens through a number of difference genres. My options are wide and rich.

Reading to Initiate Personal Change

In this category I slide down into the muddy trenches of life. These are the books for battle, the sharp weapons for putting off sin and putting on righteousness. These books help me confront and defeat personal sin and unbelief. They help me to honor God in my role as a husband and as a parent. They help me to focus on personal growth in a way that is personal, strategic, and sustained.

Our growing knowledge of God must lead to growth in conformity to Christlikeness (2 Pet. 1:5–8). Yet often we don't take the time to plan our spiritual growth. Thinking carefully about being sanctified, setting goals, and pursuing permanent life change shows the evidence of spiritual maturity. This reading category forces me to think proactively about personal growth and to determine where in my life I need to focus my attention. Carefully selected books will set the pace for focused and long-term change.

The number of great books in this category has abounded in the last decade. The church is blessed by a wealth of books on marriage, parenting, sex, depression, discontentment, stress, anxiety, fear, anger, and many others. But I often benefit from rereading some of the most helpful titles. As a parent I find much help in *Shepherding a Child's Heart* by Tedd Tripp. And I can always use a reread of the book *Running Scared: Fear, Worry, and the God of Rest* by Ed Welch. I will also read just about anything by biblical counselors David Powlison or Paul David Tripp.

How each writer approaches these topics can be wise and biblically informed—or not. And due to the spiritual dangers associated with these practical books, readers should choose them very carefully. I have seen wisely chosen books transform marriages, free sinners, and gladden grumblers. I have seen poorly chosen books feed a person's doubt, entrench a soul in legalism, and ignite a heart with self-righteousness. Specific recommendations are often best discovered under the guidance of a wise and well-read pastor who knows you.

Reading to Pursue Vocational Excellence

Christians are to work as though their boss is the Lord himself (Col. 3:23), meaning we are called to pursue vocational excellence. And working with skill requires laboring wisely and thoughtfully. I have benefitted from a selection of carefully selected business books that have helped me to do this.

For the purpose of illustrating this further from my life, I'll break this priority down into refined categories.

I read for vision. I find that my vocational life gets scattered, and I frequently need to return to a few fundamental priorities. One book that helps me narrow my focus and identify my core priories at work is *Good to Great* by Jim Collins. His point is simple: being *good* at many things prevents us from being *great* at one thing. This is an excellent book that I reread yearly. It brings clarity and focus to my main priorities at work.

I read to discover and leverage my God-given strengths. I greatly value books that help me determine personal skills. I recently read *Strengths Finder 2.0* by Tom Rath. It provided me with vision for how to restructure some of my tasks at work, to decline a few tasks that I am not skilled to handle, to rely on others to help me where I am weak, and to embrace tasks that are more aligned to my strengths. Discovering strengths always discloses weaknesses, which builds humility in my life and helps me appreciate the support roles others play around me.

I read to communicate clearly. The success of my job is closely tied to my ability to communicate clearly. Yet I'm forever beset by vagueishness. The book *Made to Stick: Why Some Ideas Survive and Others Die* by Chip and Dan Heath has helped me sharpen my writing and communicate ideas with improved stickiness.

I read to organize. No book is better at helping me organize my projects and my inbox than the book *Getting Things Done* by David Allen. If my desk and inbox are ever clean, it's because this book has taught me how to manage tasks and projects.

I read to improve my decision-making and problem-solving. I think visually, and the book *The Back of the Napkin* by Dan Roam has helped me to learn to use visual graphs to help solve problems and to develop a clear workflow. Whenever the task calls for a whiteboard and a flowchart, I open this book.

Those are a few of the books that I have read in the past eighteen months. Often my first contact with these books was at a local bookstore, but I was attracted to them because I maintain a category that keeps me alert for new books that will help me excel vocationally.

On Reading Business Books
On this topic of using secular business books, let me offer four caveats.

First, the books you read for vocational excellence may look very different from my reading list. I research and write. Perhaps you are an interior designer, an artist, a musician, a cook, a contractor, or an accountant (and if you are a mom, you may be all of these!). All of these fields will have their own corpus of vocational books that will help you grow.

Second, as with any book, a solid Christian worldview is essential when reading business books. Sins like greed, pride, self-aggrandizement, and self-promotion commonly surface in business books. Perhaps without knowing it, many business books encourage self-centered vocational pursuits. A thoughtful biblical worldview will remind us that our occupational motivations should flow from a desire to honor God and to love and serve others.

Third, pastors should never use business books as a substitute for Scripture in understanding their role as shepherds. Business books are used inappropriately by a pastor who neglects Scripture to embrace the latest business principles. The Bible is the "business book" of the pastor's "business" (shepherding).

Finally, the next hot business book is spinning off the presses as you read this sentence. A leadership or marketing guru is having his head powdered for a photo shoot that will become the cover image of a new book that promises to transform your life and job. I know how easy it is to get sucked into buying the newest books because they promise success. A perpetual chase like this will leave you exhausted (and broke). Rather, find the best books, even older books that have proven value, and read them with a discerning heart. But do read them. I believe non-Christian books can be a means of grace as we seek vocational excellence for God's glory.

Reading to Enjoy a Good Story

My final priority covers a wide terrain and includes all the books I read for leisure: non-Christian literature, novels, biographies, humor, and fantasy.

In one sense this is reading for the purpose of escape, but I am not promoting *escapism*. I do not use reading to avoid reality, but I do read to temporarily escape to another world. C. S. Lewis wrote, "Now there is a clear sense in which all reading whatever is an escape. It involves a temporary transference of the mind from our actual surroundings to things merely imagined or conceived. This happens when we read our Bible or history books, and no less when we read fiction. All such escape is *from* the same thing; immediate, concrete actuality. The important question is what we escape *to*."[9]

Christians should not blush when they read for pleasure, for escape, or "just for fun." Provided that this is not a form of escapism—and assuming the book does not glorify sin—the practice is enjoyable and honors God.

Truly, many Christians today measure their reading success with nothing more than a purely utilitarian gauge, either by how many book pages they can burn through, or by the amount of information they expose themselves to in the process. Too often we fail to read simply for pleasure. In his book on the pleasures of reading, Alan Jacobs writes, "For heaven's sake, don't turn reading into the intellectual equivalent of eating organic greens, or (shifting the metaphor slightly) some fearfully disciplined appointment with an elliptical trainer of the mind in which you count words or pages the way some people fix their attention on the 'calories burned' readout—some assiduous and taxing exercise that allows you to look back on your conquest of *Middlemarch* with grim satisfaction. How depressing. This kind of thing is not reading at all."[10] No, it's not. Or as James Sire writes in his book *How to Read Slowly*, "Reading for information only is, quite frankly, a prostitution of the art of reading."[11] It seems to me if you want to provoke writers to swing a few metaphorical punches, merely suggest that reading serves no other function than a utilitarian one.

Reading for pleasure does not mean we cannot be educated at the same time. Robert Frost once said that a good poem begins by delighting the reader and ends by bringing wisdom and clarity to the reader's life.[12] That's a great way of saying it. Samuel Johnson, in the introduction to a collection of Shakespeare's works, similarly wrote, "The end of poetry is to instruct by pleasing."[13] Good literature instructs the reader as it delights the reader, because thoughtful readers are "putting together what should never be split—excitement and knowledge, joy and truth, ecstasy and value."[14]

So sometimes I read just for pleasure. But it's not an *easy* pleasure. In explaining what motivates people to read thick, classic literature, Harold Bloom wrote,

> We read deeply for varied reasons, most of them familiar: that we cannot know enough people profoundly enough, that we need to know ourselves better; that we require knowledge, not just of self and others, but of the way things are. Yet the strongest, most authentic motive for deep reading . . . is the search for a difficult pleasure.[15]

Reading is a difficult pleasure because it requires discipline, diligence, and focus. But like in any pleasure, it is a pleasure that can be done for God's glory.

The importance of Christians reading to delight in beauty is a theme that C. S. Lewis captures well in his classic *The Screwtape Letters*, a book of fictional letters written by an experienced demon (Screwtape) to his nephew and protégé (Wormwood). The book is mostly about how to trip a young man (the "patient") and ensure he does not follow the plans of their "Enemy" (God). The book is rich in literary delight and spiritual wisdom. I highly recommend it.

At one point in the book, Screwtape chastens the young demon because he allowed his "patient" to read a book merely for the pleasure of reading it. Screwtape scolds his young protégé for his disastrous mistake: "You first of all allowed the patient to read a book he really enjoyed, because he enjoyed it and not in order to make clever remarks about it to his new friends."[16]

With that line, Lewis wants the reader to see the spiritual benefit of delighting in aesthetically beautiful books. It is a good lesson for me. I should not read merely because I have a book to write, a paper to research, a friend to impress, a blog entry to post, or a problem to solve. There is value to Christians merely reading for pleasure.

With that in mind, here are some categories I read for pleasure.

Reading the humorous. When I want to enjoy God's gift of laughter, I turn to British humorist P. G. Wodehouse. No book makes me shake my reading chair with laughter more than the collection simply titled *The Best of Wodehouse*.

Reading myth and epics. I enjoy reading ancient epic poems. Robert Fagle's modern translations of Homer's *The Odyssey* and *The Iliad* and Seamus Heaney's translation of *Beowulf* are three works I enjoy. Of course the greatest modern epic is The Lord of the Rings by J. R. R. Tolkien. If time allowed, I would march across Middle Earth annually. Escaping into this foreign land is not an escape into unreality, but is very often an escape into a more blunt form of reality. The patient Christian reader will notice many theological and ethical themes emerge as he reads (themes well captured in Peter Kreeft's *The Philosophy of Tolkien: The Worldview Behind The Lord of the Rings*). I read The Lord of the Rings primarily for pleasure, but I find that instruction trails closely behind the delight.

Reading contemporary novels. I recently read Cormac McCarthy's novel *The Road*. It is a dark novel, but it's also very thoughtful. The book shows the love between a father and son contrasted against the backdrop of a cruel and evil world. In my frequent trips to the bookstore I would say, on the whole, good contemporary non-Christian fiction is rare. McCarthy is an exception.

Reading new biographies. In the past year I've read *A. Lincoln* by Ronald C. White and *Evening in the Palace of Reason* by James Gaines. Gaines's dual biography features the brash young rationalist Frederick the Great as contrasted to the old and faith-filled Johann Sebastian Bach. This was one of my favorite reads from over the past year. Well-articulated biographies are both satisfying and instructive.

Reading historical novels. I enjoy the work of novelists who carefully handle the facts of history. These historical-novel writers can breathe life into history with a touch of fiction. This last year I read *A Voice in the Wind* by Francine Rivers, a book featuring the Christian faith in the first century Greco-Roman world, and *Killer Angels* by Michael Shaara, a historical novel of the great battle of Gettysburg during the Civil War. This genre has become one of my favorites when I read to relax in the evenings.

In all honesty, it has taken me many years to simply delight myself in beautiful books. Now they provide me with relaxation, pleasure, and a delightful weapon to foil the devil.

The Benefits of Priorities

Now that we have examined a variety of reading priorities, here are a few brief reasons why they are essential.

- *My priorities keep my library focused on the main things.* A large portion of my library is built around the person and work of Christ. This doesn't happen by accident. Reviewing this list of reading priorities reminds me of what is of primary importance. It is too easy to forget.
- *My priorities provide a comprehensive scheme for my entire reading diet.* My reading diet spans from the Bible to business books to The Lord of the Rings. I need a broad picture of all my reading, because I have a limited amount of time to read, and I must steward that time wisely. These priorities help balance my reading schedule.
- *My priorities help me determine the value of a book.* My priorities set the highest value on the rarest books (like theologically sound books on the person and work of Christ) and place the lowest priority on the most abundant literature (like best-selling secular fiction). This prevents me from allowing the abundance of literature in a category to dictate my reading diet. The categories prove valuable when I walk into a bookstore.
- *My priorities help me discern what authors are valuable on a given topic.* Many of the greatest authors pen a wide range of books. Take one of my favorite writers. Although he would be classified as a Christian writer, his understanding of the church and salvation differs widely from my theology. Yet that writer is very perceptive at explaining many other spiritual themes in the literature of Christian authors. This same author is also exceptional when explaining the basics of logic. Even some of his basic arguments in defense of Chris-

tianity are very good. So this author's books vary in value depending on what category we're talking about. Becoming a discerning reader requires that we determine which authors can be trusted in specific categories. An author that will be helpful in one category can be very unhelpful in another category.

- *My priorities help me balance proportions when the seasons of life change.* During some seasons of life I have more time to read. In other seasons I have less time. This list of priorities maintains a consistent proportion to my reading diet no matter what season I find myself in. Perhaps I have four hours to read this week and ten hours to read next week. Whether my reading time ebbs or flows, my reading priorities can remain fixed.

- *My priorities help me determine when to shelve an unfinished book.* If I choose to read a book for the purpose of spiritual reflection, but after seventy pages I find that I am not discovering reflection-worthy material, I turn to another book. These categories enable me to be strategically impatient with mediocre books and allow me to determine when a book fails to hit its intended goal in my life.

Your Turn

Now make your own list of reading priorities.

First, look at the books you have read over the last twenty-four months that have benefitted your life. Create categories for those books. Second, include any category that you don't currently read but would like to add, perhaps something mentioned in this chapter. By now you should have a list of two to five categories. Start small and be realistic. Third, begin making book selections informed by your reading priorities.

Invest the time you need to define a purpose to *why* you want to read books. Once you have an answer to this question, you will find it much easier to choose your next book from the twenty-eight million attractive options.

8

How to Read a Book

20 Tips and Tricks
for Reading Nonfiction Books

Learning to read is a miracle. As a small child, our minds begin to recognize the odd shapes on a page as letters in the alphabet. Later those letters become sounds, the sounds become words, and the words become concepts, and all because our brains can recognize letters. Today many of us can instinctively breeze past hundreds of these letters in a minute of reading. Miraculous! But no matter how well we read, we can always improve.

In this chapter I discuss twenty tips and tricks that have helped me read nonfiction books. I doubt any of my tricks are original. Many of them I learned from Mortimer Adler's seventy-year-old classic, *How to Read a Book*. Adler looks at the incremental growth of readers, from those who need training wheels to get started to mature readers who motor through complex books with confidence.

Over the years I have modified Adler's wisdom to fit my own reading habits, and I invite you to do the same with this chapter. Read my tricks, take from them what is useful, and modify them for yourself.

Speed Read

Many mature readers will grow comfortable with a broad range of reading speeds: from a quick skim of the text, to a close study of the text, to a deep meditation over the text. On one side this means training our brains to read more quickly. Learning how is not complex, and you certainly don't need a $29.99 speed-reading DVD to do it.

One simple way to read faster is by running your finger under the text as you read, increasing the speed of your finger across the page until you are pushing your eyes to read faster than normal. In other words, use your finger like a stuffed rabbit zipping along in front of a sprinting greyhound. Keep running your finger faster until you begin reading more comfortably at that speed. At first this may feel awkward, but over time, this reading speed may become easier.

Due to differing comprehension speeds, not every reader will be able to read faster. And that's okay, because a lot of books should not be read quickly. But if you can learn to read faster, go for it.

Slow Read

On the other side of the spectrum, mature readers must also be comfortable reading slowly. Book reading is not all about burning through prose. Sometimes the best way to read a book is to gear-down and read slowly and meditatively. In this situation, beware that impatience can rear its ugly head, make you feel guilty for not reading faster, and eliminate the joy from your book reading. Often our frustration with slow reading stems from a wrong attitude—of viewing books as a task to be accomplished, not as a difficult pleasure to be enjoyed.

Reading, especially when we are just getting started, can be painful. Learning to read isn't like learning to walk; it's like learning to play a piano. It's not natural.

So don't give up too easily on a book that requires slow reading. Sometimes the best books require patience. Get comfortable with the slow pace, even if it's a pace that is a lot slower than your friends'.

Install a Transmission

Mature readers know when to read quickly and when to read slowly. Reading is like driving a moving truck through mountain highways (I've done it). There are times to chug uphill in a low gear, and there are times to coast downhill in a high gear. Each book has its own terrain. Our reading speeds will change as we read, because different sections in books will be like muscling uphill or cruising downhill. Over time, you will begin to sense the terrain of a book, and you will learn how to use different gears. Just be aware that the terrain can change. Some parts of a book can be read more quickly than others. The perceptive reader can read the terrain and shift gears in response.

Anticipate

Before you begin reading a book, determine its purpose in your life. *Why* are you reading this book? What makes it better than the ten thousand books you ignored? Is it part of your spiritual diet, for personal change, or just for fun? Determining clear reading priorities is critical (see chap. 7).

Once the reading priorities are clear, then it's time to ask specific questions. I encourage readers to write five to ten specific questions they would like the author to answer. By posing questions to a book before you begin, you establish an objective basis for why you are reading this book in the first place. As you read, those questions will make it easier to determine if the book is achieving this purpose.

Determine the Author's Orbit

Which direction do you want the author to pull you? Do you want the author to pull you *into* the book (centripetal)? Or do you want the author to push you *out of* the book (centrifugal)? For example, if you read a book to simply delight in literary beauty, you want the author to *pull you in*, to hook your mind and heart with rich imagery. On the other hand, if the book is for immediate personal change, you want the author to *push you out*, so you can unhitch from the book for personal reflection and application. The force of a book is shown by how well the author moves the reader along the intended route.

Determining which direction we are seeking to move is important. The business books I read are always centrifugal, pushing me away from the book into personal reflection. The leisure books I read are often centripetal, pulling me into the book for literary delight. Knowing this difference will shape the way you read (and respond to) books.

Run a Background Check

Before I read a book, I run a quick search online to browse bookstore reviews, find concise summaries, read endorsements, and check for any high profile blurbs that have been published about the book.

This step also acquaints me with the authors I read. Who are they? Where do they work? What worldview do they represent? This critical step helps to prepare me for what I am about to read and can alert me to the author's motivations. This background check requires only a few minutes of my time, and it is time well invested.

Grab a Pen

I keep a pen behind my ear when I read, because I was a carpenter before I was a reader, and that's where all good carpenters keep pens. But I've found this habit is helpful as a reader, too. Just as I used to grab a pen before I would head to a jobsite, now I grab a pen before I head to my reading chair. I'll explain what I do with the pen a bit more in chapter 12, but for now I mention it because it is good preparation and it puts me in a posture of expectancy. Without a pen in hand, I forget the thoughts that pass through my mind. Out of habit, I grab a pen *before* I grab a book.

Slowly X-Ray the Book

Time to crack the cover for the first time and inhale that new book smell, or that old library smell—or, I guess, the warm flickering scentless pixels from your favorite e-reading device. Before I begin reading *page 1* of a book I invest thirty to sixty minutes to ask broad structural questions. Adler writes, "Every book has a skeleton hidden between its covers."[1] I am trying to x-ray for that skeletal structure.

First, I study the table of contents, noticing how chapters build on one another. Second, I scan the book and its section headings. Third, I read the chapter summaries and even the concluding chapter. Anything that looks like a concise summary gets read first. (Confession: I typically read the final page before the first page.) Then I'm ready to begin reading the introduction.

Readers are tempted to dive right into the first pages, but it takes patience to x-ray a book. The time spent slowly inspecting a book is a rewarding investment. And this step has protected me from wasting time reading mediocre books!

Take time to x-ray for the skeleton, and take as much time as you need to do it well.

Determine a Reading Strategy

After I x-ray the book for its structure, I have a good sense of the book's main points. Now I must determine *how* I want to read it. Different books must be read in different ways. Francis Bacon famously wrote, "Some books are to be tasted, others to be swallowed, and some few to be chewed and digested; that is, some books are to be read only in parts; others to be read, but not curiously; and some few to be read wholly, and with diligence and attention."[2] Very true. So what should I do with a particular book? After a slow inspection of a book I have four options:

1. **Chew and digest it like a steak**. This approach says, yes, this appears to be an excellent book that will answer the questions I have asked. I want to read the book carefully and intentionally from cover to cover.

2. **Swallow it like a milkshake**. Yes, this appears to be a helpful book that will answer my questions. I want to read the entire book, but at a quick pace. I don't want to invest too much time on this single book.

3. **Sample it like a cheese platter**. Yes and no. Portions of the book seem to be unrelated to my questions, but other sections appear to be very pertinent and helpful. There is nothing wrong with reading only portions of a book or specific chapters. By doing this you keep your book reading focused, and this focus can protect you

from losing interest. Most importantly, this choice will protect you from the common myth that books must always be read from cover to cover. Not so.

4. Spit it out like expired milk. No, this does not appear to be a book that will answer my questions, or at least not as well as another book might. I will move along and look for a replacement.

Mature readers learn to engage different books in different ways.

Jog Past the Questions

Let's say you choose option 2, to swallow the book at a quick pace. This is how I usually read nonfiction books. Now that I have a general idea about the structure of the book, it's time to read. I begin reading chapter 1, and keep moving along at a quick reading pace. If something is confusing or does not make sense to me, I make a small mark and continue reading.

In the margin of a book I mark anything that I initially disagree with or question. At the end of the chapter, I return to the marked sections. Often, by the time I have read through to the end of the chapter many of those initial questions have been answered by the author. I can save time by not stopping every time I have a question.

Note the Progression of a Chapter

As you read, pay close attention to the section headings and structural indicators like *first*, *second*, and *finally*. This internal structure is important and worth noting. If these are not marked with clear headings, you may want to make them obvious by underlining or circling them as you read along. Especially in old books and books that lack section headings, I note the structural indicators in the margin. These indicators are like street signs that guide me through the author's development of a point in a chapter. I make those markers clear.

Discover the Thesis

Every nonfiction book has a skeleton, because it has been developed from a core thesis, a sentence to summarize the author's main point.

Every chapter should also have a thesis statement. Sometimes the thesis is easy to see.

For example, in a new biography of John Calvin, the author asks in the introduction: why *another* biography of Calvin? His thesis is embedded in that single paragraph. Sometimes it's not this easy. If you can find the thesis for the book, underline it or put an asterisk in the margin. If you discover the thesis of a chapter, circle it and make a note of where you found it. Keep the thesis statement in the forefront of your mind, and watch how the author supports and defends it.

Know When to Quit

Even if you decide to read a book from cover to cover, this decision is not a vow. The evaluation of a book cannot wait until the book has been completed, and there comes a point when the reader must stop. Often a book's value (or lack of value) is clear in the first few chapters. So how far into a book should a reader go before quitting? This is where the one hundred-pages-minus-your-age rule comes in handy. This rule states that readers should start with one hundred pages and subtract their age. If you are twenty years old, you should give a book eighty pages before quitting. If you're fifty years old, give it fifty pages. The more years, the more reading experience, the less time you need before you can close and shelve a book. And it means that, when you are one hundred, you are free to judge a book by its cover.

Often readers don't stop reading because they don't have "permission" to stop. You have permission. The only book you should read entirely is the Bible. All other books must prove their value along the way. Don't allow unfinished books to pile up in a mountain of guilt. Show patience with a book, but cut the ties when necessary and move on.

Mark the Gold

I read nonfiction books in order to make discoveries, either about myself or about a particular topic. The time I invest in reading is paid back in bits of information—sometimes only paragraphs, sentences, or phrases—that change the way I live and perceive the world. It's a sweet wage for the labor. John Piper once explained it this way:

> What I have learned from about twenty-years of serious reading is this: *It is sentences that change my life, not books.* What changes my life is some new glimpse of truth, some powerful challenge, some resolution to a long-standing dilemma, and these usually come concentrated in a sentence or two. I do not remember 99% of what I read, but if the 1% of each book or article I do remember is a life-changing insight, then I don't begrudge the 99%.[3]

When 1 percent of what you read is life-transforming gold, the labor of sifting through the other 99 percent is not troublesome. Whenever I read these nuggets of gold, I mark them (I'll explain how I do this in chap. 12).

Paraphrase

Before we can embrace the author's arguments or reject the author's conclusions, we must first understand what the author said. This is the role of paraphrasing. At the end of a chapter, paraphrase the chapter's content. In one sentence, what was the main point of the chapter? At the end of the book, restate the main point in two to three sentences. The goal here is not a critique but a simple restatement (as objectively as possible) of what the author attempted to communicate.

Answer "Why?"

An author has taken time to address the topic, a publisher agreed to print it, and you bought (or borrowed) the book. So why did the author write it? Why did the publisher print it? Why did a bookstore stock it? Each of these questions must have an answer. As you read, those answers may emerge in the author's language. Your job as a reader is to find the answers. Often an evaluation of a book is informed by answering these important *why* questions.

Find the Holes

It takes discernment to evaluate *what the author has written*, but it requires advanced discernment to determine *what the author has left unwritten.* Often a book's fatal flaw is not that the author said something poorly, but that the author failed to say something essential. What was left unsaid? What pieces were missing from the book? The questions that you write out before you begin reading become very useful at this point. By returning to your initial questions, you can determine if the author missed anything on the topic.

Let the Dust Settle

After you have completed a book, stop and give yourself time before making a final evaluation. Like driving a pickup down a gravel road, reading a book kicks up a lot of dust (details) in the brain, and it's helpful to let the dust settle before we evaluate the book. Often the book's value will become clearer after a few days, after your mind has processed the details. The thoughts that linger in your mind about a book are the thoughts that you want to capture. Go back and write those thoughts in the inside cover of the book or in a notebook.

Compare and Contrast Books

If we select books with specific priorities in mind, we will inevitably read books with overlapping content. Mature readers compare their books. After reading, answer a few more questions in the front cover, such as: Is this book better or worse than the other books I have read on the topic? Is it more helpful or less helpful? Where did this book contradict another book? What content was covered that other books neglected? The best books, the books that cover a topic well, are the books we respect, cherish, reread, and recommend to our friends.

Collect and Store the Gold

Some people collect coins and baseball cards. I collect other people's thoughts. When I read an important sentence or paragraph (the 1 percent), I mark it and then later return and copy it into a topical database on my computer.

If you have a poor memory (like me) you will need a place to collect the sentences and paragraphs that you hope to retain for the future. How exactly you go about collecting these insights may look different. Some readers use a photocopier and folders. Others use a handwritten journal. I use a simple Microsoft Excel database. I collect quotes, which I type out verbatim, and organize by topical categories. I can tell you from personal experience, a captured thought that later finds expression in a real-life situation will boost a desire within you to continue reading. Whatever process works for you, find a way to store the gold.

What about Reading Scripture?

Those twenty tips and tricks are great for reading nonfiction books. Often when I talk about these tricks, there comes a point when someone will say, "Yes, thanks for the suggestions, but I want to read my *Bible* better. How can I do this?" Great question.

Honestly, I think we read our Bibles poorly because we read all of our nonfiction books poorly. To better read our Bibles, or any nonfiction book, we must work to improve our reading skills. Sharpening our reading skills will improve how we read and how we benefit from all our nonfiction books—including the most important Book of them all.

By pursuing self-discipline and seeking to excel in reading books, we continue to build off our years of foundational reading experience. From learning the ABCs as children to pursuing greater degrees of literacy as adults, we celebrate the amazing miracle we call reading.

9

Literature Is Life

Tapping into the Benefits of Fiction Literature

Novels are deadly poison to the soul.

Or at least this has been the warning sounded from some pulpits. Take Scottish pastor Horatius Bonar, one of the nineteenth-century's greatest preachers and writers. He preached a cross-centered gospel, he wrote Christ-centered hymns, and he authored a set of devotionals that are still being printed. But he was no fan of contemporary fiction. In 1861 he wrote the book *Follow the Lamb; or, Counsels to Converts*. His advice to new believers:

> Shun novels; they are the literary curse of the age; they are to the soul what ardent [enthusiastic] spirits are to the body. If you be a parent, keep novels out of the way of your children. But whether you be a parent or not, neither read them yourself, nor set an example of novel-reading to others. Don't let novels lie on your table, or be seen in your hand, even in a railway carriage. The 'light reading for the rail' has done deep injury to many a young man and woman. The light literature of the day is working a world of harm; vitiating the taste of the young, enervating their minds, unfitting them for life's plain work, eating out their love of the Bible, teaching them

a false morality, and creating in the soul an unreal standard of truth, and beauty, and love.[1]

A pastoral lashing like this over the dangers of fictional literature was not unique to the nineteenth century. Nor were these lashings entirely unwarranted, given what I now know about the superficial "light reading" in Scotland at the time.

Yet at the same time Bonar was encouraging new Christians to shun novels like the plague, a Russian novelist nearly 1,500 miles away was just beginning to hit stride.

By the time his life was over, Fyodor Dostoyevsky would alter how Christians evaluated novels. He would be remembered as one of the greatest novelists of all time, and according to theologian J. I. Packer, the greatest Christian storyteller who ever lived.[2] And behind this high praise is the assumption that novels are a fitting way to capture the Christian life. I agree. And not only are Christian novels valuable, so too are classic novels by non-Christians.

The Value of Fictional Literature

From the start of this chapter, let me note that I write as a student. To appreciate fictional literature I rely heavily on wise scholars, and none of them more than Leland Ryken. Read Ryken's books, and you will learn a lot.

In perhaps one of his lesser-known books, Ryken writes a brief summary of the many benefits Christians can expect from the pages of fiction:

> Literature is a form of discovery, perception, intensification, expression, interpretation, creativity, beauty, and understanding. These are ennobling activities and qualities. For a Christian, they can be God-glorifying, a gift from God to the human race to be accepted with zest.[3]

Let me unpack this.

Fictional literature can help us explore abstract human experiences. In chapter 5, I mentioned that each of us participates in a brotherhood of humanity. And because we share similar experiences, writers of different eras, cultures, and even worldviews can connect with us at a profound level. The best fictional authors spell out our common human experience in ways that prove elusive to other forms of writing. Which is to say, fictional literature may prove at times to be more true than nonfiction. Novels are free to move beyond the particulars of history to the universals of human experience, to such abstract and philosophical concepts as love, hate, goodness, and evil. With such liberty, the author may probe the human condition more profoundly. Tapping into the soul of human experience, the writer spins a web of believability that is potentially more convincing than the historical account. As the plot thickens, the reader identifies with the probable experience of the fictional characters. The invented story serves to usher the reader into the most important realms of reality.[4]

Fictional literature can deepen our appreciation for concrete human experience. By retelling life with words, novelists heighten our sensitivity to common human experiences. Literature gives a depth to human experience and natural beauty. God has gifted authors to focus our attention on things that we take for granted— like the sun-glistened water droplets on a leaf after a hard spring rain—and these images intensify our experience of the world we see around us.

Fictional literature expands our range of experiences. We get one chance at this life. We have one body, one mind, and one life to live. Reading provides us with a vicarious experience of others' lives. Literature introduces us to the lives and experiences and thoughts and affections of others, even if those characters are the product of an author's wild imagination. By doing so, literature expands our own experiences and causes us to grow in our sympathy toward others. Through literature we can taste the life experiences of those who live in lands that are distant, cultures that are distinct, and in generations that are now extinct.

Fictional literature provides beauty and creativity to be enjoyed. The best fiction is beautiful, and this beauty finds its origin in God's beauty. We discover beautiful literature because our

Creator has endowed our world with artists who reflect the beauty that originates in him. This beautiful literature can be enjoyed for the glory of God even if it comes from the fingertips of a non-Christian, Christians can and *should* read literature simply for the pleasure of it. C. S. Lewis made this point in chapter 7. By appreciating the beauty of literature, we honor God, the Giver of all beauty.

Those are a few reasons why we should embrace fiction "with zest." But reading fiction takes skill, so here are some important points to keep in mind.

(Mis)Reading Fiction

Obviously, reading fiction is different from reading nonfiction. Readers misread fiction when they expect to learn propositions, or discover a thesis. Too often nonfiction readers (like me) speed-read literature in search of the propositional truth claims. Fictional literature frustrates impatient readers who scan only for propositions. Of course literature does at times embody propositional truths, but this should not be our primary reason for reading literature. Reading literature is about absorption, about being lost in a story, and about delighting in the beautiful prose of a gifted writer. Fiction is art, and it must be handled differently from a business book. As novelist Flannery O'Connor said, "The fact is, people don't know what they are expected to do with a novel, believing, as so many do, that art must be utilitarian, that it must do something, rather than be something."[5]

Specifically, we misread fiction when we approach it with the hope that it will shape our worldview. In chapter 4, I argued that Scripture alone should inform our worldview. A Christian reader may view the world through biblical eyes, but this vision is not necessarily learned through fiction. Literature can help us appreciate the beauty of the biblical worldview, and it can provide examples of the biblical worldview at work, but it cannot shape the main components of a Christian worldview. It shouldn't be asked to. This is the task of Scripture.

Sowing Grace in Dark Soil

We may not read literature to discover propositional truth claims or to develop a Christian worldview, yet we must remember that every author writes from a worldview, however complete or partial it appears.

The best Christian novelists write from a biblical worldview, one that is not afraid of digging into the soil of common human experience. O'Connor once addressed what she called "sorry" Christian fiction:

> Ever since there have been such things as novels, the world has been flooded with bad fiction for which the religious impulse has been responsible. The sorry religious novel comes about when the writer supposes that because of his belief, he is somehow dispensed from the obligation to penetrate concrete reality. He will think that the eyes of the Church or of the Bible or of his particular theology have already done the seeing for him, and that his business is to rearrange this essential vision into satisfying patterns, getting himself as little dirty in the process as possible. His feeling about this may have been made more definite by one of those Manichean-type theologies which sees the natural world as unworthy of penetration. But the real novelist, the one with an instinct for what he is about, knows that he cannot approach the infinite directly, that he must penetrate the natural human world as it is.[6]

In other words, good Christian fiction plants the seeds of grace deep in the soil of realism and common human experience. The best Christian novels grow out of the manure of this fallen world.

F(r)iction

The soil of this world is sinful. We live in a world filled with disgusting acts of selfishness, brutality, and abuse. This is because the world is populated with dark, sinful hearts—hearts like ours. Our world groans to be freed from the chaos of sin. So do we. And the gospel answers our longing to be freed from sin. Christian literature uses the sin-stained world as the soil where the green sprout of grace grows.

This fact explains why even the Bible includes stories that involve sins like adultery, witchcraft, lying, and murder. Ryken writes,

> Like all literature, [the Bible] portrays life as we know it in a fallen world. Many of the experiences about which we read in the Bible are sordid, evil, and repulsive. This is no reason to avoid reading the Bible. Some literature does, indeed, offer evil for the reader's approval and should be judged as immoral for doing so. But the portrayal of objectionable behavior or attitudes does not by itself mean that the book as a whole approves of these things.[7]

In other words, the *appearance of sin* in a book does not mean the author is *approving of sin*. Scripture is our model. The Bible uses sin to magnify God's holiness, mercy, and grace. This depiction of sin is what O'Connor calls the price of restoration.[8] The price of restoration is gaining clarity about the depth of sin and depravity in the human heart and the world. Christian novelist Larry Woiwode said in an interview, "If sin isn't mentioned or depicted, there's no need for redemption. How can the majesty of God's mighty arm be defined in a saccharin romance?"[9]

Ryken, O'Connor, and Woiwode have a point, and it's a very sticky point. God's "amazing grace" is especially displayed when it "saves a wretch." To some degree, the author must paint a picture of the wretchedness of sin in order for grace to emerge in its brilliance. Thus, grace-filled literature is often not "clean" literature. In fact, God's redemptive grace is hard to capture in "clean" fiction. This is especially true of conversion stories, because conversion is about contrast.

So how much sin is required for the contrast to become clear? What type of realism is permissible in fiction? Where are the lines drawn? These are very difficult questions, and the gutters are deep on both sides of the street. On the one side of the road, we cannot merely shut our eyes to depictions of sin and evil in literature. We find depictions of evil in the Bible. On the other side of the road, we cannot affirm fiction that glorifies sin or applauds unbelief.

So how *much* freedom should Christian novelists be given in their depictions of sin? That is a question that remains tough to answer. Like so many areas of life, sensible and discerning readers must listen carefully to their own consciences.

Sin as Sin

Christian novelists depict sin differently than non-Christian novelists. O'Connor writes, "The Christian novelist is distinguished from his pagan colleagues by recognizing sin as sin. According to this heritage, he sees it not as a sickness or an accident of environment, but as a responsible choice against God which involves his eternal future."[10] In fact Christians will observe more evil, because "writers who see by the light of their Christian faith will have, in these times, the sharpest eyes for the grotesque, for the perverse, and for the unacceptable."[11]

So how does the author view mankind? Does the author understand the sinfulness of the human condition? Does the author understand that man is in a predicament for which he needs a savior, even if that savior is a poor echo of the Living Savior?

A non-Christian author who has at least some understanding of the gravity of personal sin will write differently than the author who is ignorant of the gravity and consequences of personal sin. This same distinction is true in movies. Grant Horner writes,

> Perhaps the single most important philosophical question to ask when watching a film is, "What is the nature of humanity according to this movie?" If one's view of the nature of man (in theological terms, "anthropology") is skewed, then everything else will be off. I cannot possibly emphasize this enough: anthropology is the key. Error at this point inevitably leads to greater error in many other places. Every film contains presuppositions—and most contain overt statements—about the nature of mankind. The spectrum is deceptively simple: man is good, man is bad, man is both, man can change categories, or man is morally neutral (i.e., categories of good and bad are fictional or somehow irrelevant). . . . The real issue is, what is the overall view of the nature of man presented by the film as seen by a reasonably perceptive viewer? This can largely be determined by considering plot, characterization, and the tone or mood of the film.[12]

The same principle can be carried over into discerning fiction books. Authors that are most aware of man's sinful depravity—whether or not they call it *depravity*—are the novelists that are most in tune with the reality of this world.

Embrace the Subtle Good

Great novelists are honest about the evil of this world, but they are also perceptive to the subtle graces and the quiet beauty in this world. Goodness is often more difficult to portray than wickedness, says P. D. James. She should know. James is a crime novelist, a Christian, and the author of the thriller, *The Children of Men*. In an interview in the 1980s, James said,

> I suppose that wickedness reveals itself often in action. Goodness also does, but on a quieter plane. Good people often reveal their goodness through the whole of the quiet revelation of their character in the ordinary events of life. And if a good person is being courageous he's probably being courageous in facing rather ordinary troubles—sick children, a sick wife, an uncongenial job. Wicked people are murdering. It's more dramatic. Goodness is very seldom dramatic, I think. And it's much more easy to write about drama.[13]

Evil is dramatic, easy to communicate, and in full view of the reader. *Integrity* is subtle, more difficult to communicate, and often passes unnoticed by the reader.

The cunning scheme of a mob boss in criminal fiction, the bloodthirsty murder by a vampire in horror books, or the illicit sexual encounter by two people in a romance novel are far less demanding of the reader's attention than the subtle fruit of the Holy Spirit. The grace and beauty that we read in Christian novels are much more subtle and thereby much more demanding on the reader's careful perception. And this is because appreciating grace and integrity and goodness requires the reader to detect the subtleties.

In literature, the best authors help us see and appreciate love, joy, peace, patience, kindness, goodness, faithfulness, gentleness, and self-control (Gal. 5:22–23). As Christian readers we must read with patience and skill to appreciate the subtle goodness of God's presence when it appears.

Starting Point

It's that time in the chapter for another confession.

For many years I *avoided* fictional literature. At some point I began *tolerating* fiction being in my house (infiltrated by my wife). Now I can honestly say that I *enjoy* fiction.

So what caused this fictional conversion? The defining book in my shift from opposition to embrace can be traced back to my reading of Leland Ryken's book *Realms of Gold: The Classics in Christian Perspective*.[14]

In *Realms of Gold,* Ryken guided me through the classics of literature: *The Odyssey* by Homer; *Canterbury Tales* by Chaucer; *Macbeth* by Shakespeare; *Paradise Lost* by Milton; *The Scarlet Letter* by Hawthorne; *Great Expectations* by Dickens; *The Death of Ivan Illych* by Tolstoy; and *The Stranger* by Camus. Ryken's guidance opened my eyes to the value of classic literature in the Christian life. And as I write this book, Ryken is working on individual guides to classics of literature like these (forthcoming from Crossway). I will be buying them all.

If classic novels sound intimidating, though, don't be embarrassed to begin with children's fiction. As I was getting started, I was greatly helped by The Chronicles of Narnia series by C. S. Lewis. I think every Christian home should have a set, and every Christian adult should read them regularly![15]

Literature Is Life

Since nearly everything I have learned about reading literature from a Christian perspective has come from the pen of Ryken, it is fitting to conclude this brief chapter with his summary of the value—and the limitations—of fiction literature.

> Literature is life. If you want to know what, deep down, people feel and experience, you can do no better than read the stories and poems of the human race. Writers of literature have the gift

of observing and then expressing in words the essential experiences of people.

The rewards of reading literature are significant. Literature helps to humanize us. It expands our range of experiences. It fosters awareness of ourselves and the world. It enlarges our compassion for people. It awakens our imaginations. It expresses our feelings and insights about God, nature, and life. It enlivens our sense of beauty. And it is a constructive form of entertainment.

Christians should neither undervalue nor overvalue literature. It is not the ultimate source of truth. But it clarifies the human situation to which the Christian faith speaks. It does not replace the need for the facts that science and economics and history give us. But it gives us an experiential knowledge of life that we need just as much as those facts.

Literature does not always lead us to the City of God. But it makes our sojourn on earth much more a thing of beauty and joy and insight and humanity.[16]

10

Too Busy to Read

Six Ways to Find (and Protect) the Time You Need to Read Books

Hopefully by now you are motivated to read books. Great! But where will you find the time? A lack of free time is the leading cause of book neglect, and we don't need a scientific study to prove it. Reading a book is time-intensive, and for most of us, spare time is hard to find. But it can be found. This is the story of how I find (and protect) the time I need to read books.

One Ordinary Man's Story

I read a lot of books. My annual goal is to read seventy-five books, which may sound like a lot. And it is a lot, but not compared to some of my extraordinary friends.

So how do I read seventy-five books each year? Let's start with a few calculations.

First, I don't read a lot of books because I'm smart. Evidence weighs heavily to the contrary. I spent the first two years in college on academic probation and nearly got kicked out of a public university for poor grades. I'd love to forget this, but I find it helpful as a bludgeoning cudgel to smack my pride in the nose. For me, learning is unnatural.

Second, I don't read a lot of books because I have a ton of free time. My calendar is full, my honey-do list is long, my three kids are hyper, and my boss is active (or is it the other way around?). And my running shoes are neglected, my weight bench is dusty, and my yard is overgrown. I live in the real world, just like you.

The short answer is that I find the time to read because I invest my time carefully. Sometimes I read over my morning plate of scrambled eggs; sometimes I read over my lunchtime can of tuna salad; and sometimes I read over my cup of evening tea. I read at the DMV when I renew my driver's license. I read in airports and in jets as I travel for work. I read when I'm waiting on my barber. I read books to my kids. Sometimes I read when the kids are climbing all over my back on the living room floor. And on my day off, I retreat for a couple hours to read at a local coffee shop. All of this "found time," added up, equals books read.

Words Per Minute

But just how much time do we need to read books? Since I took the same college algebra class three times, I can run a few mathematical equations for you.

First, most people can find sixty minutes each day to read. It sounds like a lot, but it really isn't: fifteen minutes in the morning, fifteen minutes at lunchtime, and another thirty minutes in the evening. No problem. At this pace, you can devote seven hours to reading each week (or 420 minutes).

The average reader moves through a book at a pace of about 250 words per minute. So 420 minutes of reading per week translates into 105,000 words per week. This book is roughly 55,000 words. Assuming that you can read for one hour each day, and that you read at around 250 words per minute, you can complete more than one book per week, or about seventy books per year.

Some weeks will provide more, or less, time for reading. But by carving little pockets of time throughout your week and by using your time well, it is not impossible to read a hefty stack of books each year.

So how to find those pockets of reading time in the first place? Here are some tips that have helped me.

Expect War

When we set out to read important books, we can expect opposition from our hearts. Reading is a discipline, and all disciplines require self-discipline, and self-discipline is the one thing our sinful flesh will resist.

Our spirit may be eager to read a book, but our flesh is weak. Our flesh would rather self-indulge on passive entertainment. Movies and television can be wonderful gifts from God if we use them wisely, but unchecked they will hijack our schedules and rob us of our reading time. Book reading is not just a matter of time management; it's a matter of warfare. Wherever sinful self-indulgence dominates our free time, we can be certain that personal idols are at work in our flesh, seeking to divide and conquer the soul (1 Pet. 2:11).

Idols of entertainment and pleasure make the discipline of book reading a battle with our flesh. We'd rather avoid discipline and be occupied with easier tasks like e-mail, Internet browsing, and movies. We neglect books because our hearts reject the discipline required to read them. And that is a spiritual problem, a lack of personal discipline, not a lack of time. And until we apply the sin-freeing gospel to our own hearts—and the idols therein—we may never cultivate the self-discipline required to read books. Our flesh wars within us. If we don't kill the idols of laziness and self-indulgence, these idols will kill our literacy.

So expect a fight from your flesh.

Make Time, Not Excuses

In 1964 Robert Lee calculated the leisure time available to Americans. In his research he compared the leisure time available to modern Americans to the leisure time available to an average American worker in the mid-1800s. What did Lee discover?

It is a striking fact to note that the working man of a century ago spent some seventy hours per week on the job and lived about forty years. Today he spends some forty hours per week at work and can expect to live about seventy years. This adds something like twenty-two more *years of leisure* to his life, about 1,500 free hours each year, and a total of some 33,000 additional free hours that the man born today has to enjoy![1]

That is a stunning amount of free time! So why is this leisure time so elusive when it comes to finding the time we need to read books?

For many of us, reading is more a lack of of desire than of a lack of free time. C. S. Lewis wrote, "The only people who achieve much are those who want knowledge so badly that they seek it while the conditions are still unfavorable. Favorable conditions never come."[2] The same is true of reading. Favorable conditions for reading books never come.

There are always interruptions and other things to do. We can all find excuses for why we cannot read: we're too busy, we're too tired, we're too burned out from the day, we're too _____ (you fill in the blank). But we all find time to do what we "want" to do. The problem is not that we don't have *time* to read, but that we don't have the *desire* to read. So learn to love reading—because it's easier to find time to do what you love to do.

Read Great Books

How do we cultivate that love? Start by researching and finding the very best books available. Ask your friends for recommendations. Great books can be found in every genre, from novels that grab your heart with the twists and turns of a brilliant plot, or history books that open your imagination to experience decisive moments in the world, or Christian living books that bring clarity to your soul and focus to your life. Nothing cultivates a love of reading more than a steady diet of great books.

I think the only books that should be burned—or at least banned— are mediocre ones. Find books that grab you. Read the books that make you lose sleep at night. Perhaps that's a book that you have already read. Reread it.

Aim to become a reader who sits down late in the evening after a long day and grabs for a book to relax. This is a reader who *loves* to read! You may not be there yet, reading may be a chore, and television and movies and browsing the Internet might hold more sway over your leisure time. Press on. Keep searching for great books.

Set Reading Priorities

Our reading may not be disciplined, efficient, or fruitful until we read with purpose. Before you begin reading a book, determine *why* you are reading it.

We will often neglect what we don't prioritize. And book reading is often neglected because it fails to be a priority; and it fails to be a priority because we have not defined our reading goals clearly. Once we define the purpose of our reading, it becomes much easier to see the practical value of books in our lives.

We discussed how to establish personal reading priorities in chapter 7. Factor everything you *want* to read and *need* to read—even factor in your *fun* reading. Then choose books that align with those priorities.

Stop Something

But for all the extra leisure time available, we each have a limited number of days in our lives (Psalm 90). The brevity of life requires that we limit our priorities. Are you still waiting for the time to read? You may need to stop doing something else. Novelist Alan Bissett understands this. He wrote,

> The reader is under assault from hundreds of television channels, 3D cinema, a computer-gaming business so large it dwarfs Hollywood, iPhones, Wii, YouTube, free commuter newspapers, an engorged celebrity culture, instant access to all the music ever recorded, 24-hour sports news, and DVD box-sets of shows such as *The Wire*, *Mad Men* and *Lost* that replicate some of the scope and depth of literature. Unprecedented levels of consumer debt, and now a recession, have seen everyone working longer hours. A leisure time that was already precious has been chewed into by text-messaging, Facebook and emails. Almost everyone I speak

to claims that they "love books but just can't find the time to read." Well, they probably could—they're just choosing to spend it differently.[3]

What competes for your reading time? What is less important than your reading? Nothing squanders time away more than pursuing things without a purpose. And given that the average American adult (18–34) invests only 10 minutes each day reading, yet watches 116 minutes of television, I think many of us have time that we can spend differently.[4]

So what in your life needs to *stop* happening so that reading can *start* happening?

Read Three Books at a Time

Having trouble finding reading time? It may be that you need to read more books. Seriously. A curious thing happened in my own life. I discovered that when I began reading three books at a time, I found more time to read. Why? It's pretty simple, actually. I found that different times in my day allowed me to read different types of books.

I enjoy reading historical novels, but I don't read a historical novel right after I roll out of bed in the morning. I enjoy reading theology, but I rarely read theology at night before I go to bed. I enjoy reading long epics like Lord of the Rings, but I can't get into an epic novel while traveling.

Different genres are suited for different times, and having three books from different genres gives me greater flexibility in capturing fragments of time throughout the day. On the other hand, reading only one book makes it harder to find time to read, because it restricts the number of contexts. Let me explain.

Save the Environment

When I started thinking about the situations where I seek to capture reading fragments, I began to see that certain settings favored certain types of books. Here are a few of those places:

Desk reading. I haul myself out of bed, pour some coffee, and head downstairs to my desk. Here is where I meet with God through Scripture and often where I dive into commentaries on the Bible and theology. Most of my serious devotional reading is done at that desk in the early morning hours.

Coffee shop reading. The longest and most difficult books, the books that require the most caffeinated attention, I bring to the coffee shop on my days off. There I invest between two and four hours reading with singular focus. Once the ear buds are in place, the music begins, and the cover is opened, the world around me fades away.

Barbershop reading. My barber has twenty magazine subscriptions, because people waiting for him have free time to read. I never go to the barbershop without a book. I find that I can read just about any type of book in this setting.

Lunch-break reading. At work I can often read a brief devotional in small fragments of time. I keep an array of books within arm's reach at work, including a copy of *The Valley of Vision* at my desk. I often take fifteen minutes during my lunch break for a brief devotional. It's a great time to recalibrate my heart in the middle of the day.

Evening "my-fried-is-brain" reading. At night when the sun is down, the kids are asleep, and my brain is shot from the day, I like to read historical novels and biographies. For me this is the best time to read the lives of others.

Bedside reading. In defiance of *feng shui* experts, I keep a stack of books next to my bed. These are books that I read in the thirty minutes before I fall asleep, and each of the books can be read in short chunks. These are *not* books I intend to read from cover-to-cover. These are my cheese platter samplers, the books with selected chapters I want to read, or books of short poems, or thrilling books that I dip into occasionally. This stack of books never gets read completely, because it's a stack of books that I have no intention to read completely in the first place. I replace the stack of books every couple of months.

Travel reading. I travel a bit. But it took me a while to figure out how to make the most of my travel reading. For a while I traveled with light fiction, thinking that a novel would be perfect. But my reading never got any lift. While trying to read novels in the vibrating hum of a jet fuselage, I found myself nodding off and losing interest. Later I discovered that at thirty thousand feet, my life seems to come into perfect focus. Once I made this discovery, I began to limit my carry-on to business books, Christian living books, and books that gave me just enough instruction to stimulate reflection and planning about my family, my job, and my life priorities. I step off the jet with pages of thoughtful personal reflection, a renewed energy for life, and a clear focus on my primary goals.

By reading multiple books at the same time, I have the flexibility to read certain books in certain settings. I'm sure your reading priorities and your reading environments will differ from mine. But think carefully about these environments, because each environment will favor certain types of reading.

The Point

The main point of this chapter is that we can find the time necessary to read books. But this requires thought on a number of related topics.

- Expect resistance from your heart.
- Make time to read, not excuses for why you don't read. We all have good excuses.
- Cultivate a hunger for books by reading (and rereading) great books.
- Set your reading priorities, and let them drive your book selections.
- Stop doing something else in order to make time to read.
- Try reading three (or more) books at a time and take advantage of your environments.

You don't need to be a professional book reviewer to read a lot of books. And you don't need to be brilliant either. But you do need to be purposeful and consistent. And if you can discipline yourself, you will find the time you need to read.

11

Driven to Distraction

How Internet Habits Cripple Book Reading

Meet David Ulin. David is the book editor for the *Los Angeles Times*. David reads a lot of books because he gets paid to review a lot of books. It's David's job.

But one day David noticed something alarming—the task of reading books was becoming more and more difficult. That's bad news for a professional book reader.

The problem was not the lack of will to read, but the lack of concentration. He wrote about his experience in the autobiographical article, "The Lost Art of Reading":

> Reading is an act of contemplation, perhaps the only act in which we allow ourselves to merge with the consciousness of another human being. . . . In order for this to work, however, we need a certain type of silence, an ability to filter out the noise. Such a state is increasingly elusive in our over-networked culture, in which every rumor and mundanity is blogged and tweeted. Today, it seems it is not contemplation we seek but an odd sort of distraction masquerading as being in the know. Why? Because of the illusion that illumination is based on speed, that it is more important to

react than to think, that we live in a culture in which something is attached to every bit of time.[1]

Ulin pointed to the Internet as a primary cause of his withering concentration. And he is not alone. In the summer of 2008 journalist Nicholas Carr published an article in *The Atlantic* that brought these concerns to popular attention under the provoking title, "Is Google Making Us Stupid?" He wrote,

> Over the past few years I've had an uncomfortable sense that someone, or something, has been tinkering with my brain, remapping the neural circuitry, reprogramming the memory. My mind isn't going—so far as I can tell—but it's changing. I'm not thinking the way I used to think. I can feel it most strongly when I'm reading. Immersing myself in a book or a lengthy article used to be easy. My mind would get caught up in the narrative or the turns of the argument, and I'd spend hours strolling through long stretches of prose. That's rarely the case anymore. Now my concentration often starts to drift after two or three pages. I get fidgety, lose the thread, begin looking for something else to do. I feel as if I'm always dragging my wayward brain back to the text. The deep reading that used to come naturally has become a struggle. . . . And what the Net seems to be doing is chipping away my capacity for concentration and contemplation. My mind now expects to take in information the way the Net distributes it: in a swiftly moving stream of particles. Once I was a scuba diver in the sea of words. Now I zip along the surface like a guy on a Jet Ski.[2]

Carr and Ulin sound oddly similar. So what is happening to them? And is this happening to us?

To answer these questions we need to address how online reading habits damage our offline reading habits.

Socially, the Internet offers us streams of fragmented information that must be quickly browsed as they pass. Social media (like Facebook and Twitter) and online browsing patterns will train our minds to hunt for information in small, isolated bits. In fact "reading in the traditional open-ended sense is not what most of us, whatever our age and level of computer literacy, do on the Internet," writes

Susan Jacoby. "What we are engaged in—like birds of prey looking for their next meal—is a process of swooping around with an eye out for certain kinds of information."³ Whether our brains are being rewired as a result is a topic of debate. What is less debated is that browsing fragments of information erodes concentration. And this erosion in concentration influences how we think and how we read books.

Ironically, these concerns echo a very old fear voiced by an ancient philosopher.

Danger! Books Ahead

So far in this book I have assumed that books are good for us. You've probably decided to read this book based upon the same assumption. Who would have the audacity to question the value of books? The Greek philosopher Socrates.

Socrates resisted the idea of books. He sought to preserve a society that was structured around oral communication. Socrates lost the debate, of course, but why was he provoked by the arrival of books? The reasons are several, but I want to focus on two of them:

- Socrates feared written books would weaken the human memory.
- Socrates feared written books would weaken deep thinking.⁴

In Socrates's opinion, books would undermine the oral tradition of the scholars, and the loss of the oral tradition would lead to shriveled minds. And when you think about it, his concern is reasonable. If we are honest, we admit that we don't write things down to *remember* them; usually we write things down to *forget* them. Once we have information written on paper, we have little need to memorize the particulars and less need to train our minds to recall the details. From this angle, books would do the remembering, making the human memory less necessary, and thereby weakening the minds of scholars. In quoting from a story he had himself internalized, Socrates said:

> If men learn this [writing], it will implant forgetfulness in their souls; they will cease to exercise memory because they will rely on that

which is written, calling things to remembrance no longer from within themselves, but by means of external marks; what you have discovered is a recipe not for memory, but for reminder.[5]

Socrates was concerned that scholars would rely on external details found in books rather than pursue deep thought and meditation. He was concerned with *externalized knowledge* replacing *internalized wisdom*. The oral tradition encouraged a healthy fostering of *internal wisdom*; libraries of books would become crutches of *external reminders*.

I'm not sure if Socrates was aware of the tremendous benefits of books—including preserving his own words about books (ironic). But it was clear that Socrates saw the dawn of books as the dusk of the human memory.

The dangers that Socrates foresaw have now arrived in the modern Internet. When we can access the sum total of human knowledge with one thumb on a smartphone in 0.2 seconds through a Google search as we drive 70 mph down the freeway, what happens to the human memory? Who needs to remember details? The memory shrinks like a grape my kids left in the backseat of the car.

An honest *Wired* magazine writer confessed, "The line between where my memory leaves off and Google picks up is getting blurrier by the second."[6] That was a chief concern of Socrates. As online search engines become highly refined mechanisms for finding information, our internal memory becomes less necessary. We make decisions based upon *access to external reminders* rather than from an *internal storehouse of cultivated wisdom*.

The implications are huge for book readers: how we read online affects how we read offline.

Christian book readers who frequently use the Internet and social media will be faced with four temptations that will make it difficult to preserve and cultivate book reading skills.

Four Temptations

Fragmented Browsing vs. Sustained Comprehension
The Internet is designed to encourage us to browse information, not to slowly read and digest it. Carr writes, "Most of the proprietors

of the commercial Internet have a financial stake in collecting the crumbs of data we leave behind as we flit from link to link—the more crumbs, the better. The last thing these companies want is to encourage leisurely reading or slow, concentrated thought. It's in their economic interest to drive us to distraction."[7]

And we like distraction. We want distraction. Distraction is how we stay busy enough to avoid the self-discipline required to read books. In light of what he calls our "fully-wired and over-stimulated postmodern world of cell phones, radios, laptops, video games, omnipresent television, extreme sports, and much else," Christian philosopher Douglas Groothuis writes:

> The compulsive search for diversion is often an attempt to escape the wretchedness of life. We have great difficulty being quiet in our rooms, when the television or computer screen offers a riot of possible stimulation. Postmodern people are perpetually restless; they frequently seek solace in diversion instead of satisfaction in truth. As Pascal said, "Our nature consists in movement; absolute rest is death." The postmodern condition is one of oversaturation and over-stimulation, and this caters to our propensity to divert ourselves from pursuing higher realities.[8]

The Internet offers us a riot of stimulation to keep us from these "higher realities." The Internet presents random fragments of information that flow at us in a stream—a Facebook status update, a new Tweet, even a random email—and attention gets chopped up into small, disconnected fragments throughout the day. The Internet encourages superficial browsing, not concentration.

Book reading, on the other hand, cannot happen without disciplined and sustained linear concentration. Instead of browsing for fragments of information, we must learn to become deep thinkers who work hard to comprehend (2 Tim. 2:7).

Success in life demands that we cultivate the skill of sustained linear reasoning. This is true of reading books; and it's true of learning mathematics, playing music, solving complex personal problems, and making important decisions. Reading is a way to preserve and cultivate the sustained linear concentration we need for life.

If we fill our lives with fragments of information, our brains will adapt and our concentration will weaken. We will begin to find articles, chapters, and books increasingly demanding as our attention spans shrivel. Eventually we will find it difficult to stroll through long stretches of prose.

Book readers must work to sharpen their attention. Like marathon runners who train daily to stretch their endurance, book readers must discipline themselves to read *one book* for thirty to sixty or ninety minutes at a time, struggling to increase their mental concentration. This will be impossible unless there are times when we are unplugged from the fragmented distractions of life.

Reacting vs. Thinking

Traditionally, a reader selected one book and sat alone in a reading chair. When great ideas were encountered, the reader internalized those ideas and reflected on them. If the reader encountered points of disagreement, the reader also stopped to reflect on what made the point disagreeable. In other words, traditional readers engaged with a book and engaged their thinking.

This has changed with online social interaction. Now, when we come across an idea that we like, we are tempted to quickly react, to share the idea with friends in an e-mail, on Facebook, or on a blog. When we disagree, our initial response is to ask for the input of others. With online access to so many friends, the temptation is to react, not to ponder, and it's a problem Kevin Kelly notices. In his article "Reading in a Whole New Way" he compares reading from a book page to reading from a screen.

> Books were good at developing a contemplative mind. Screens encourage more utilitarian thinking. A new idea or unfamiliar fact will provoke a reflex to do something: to research the term, to query your screen "friends" for their opinions, to find alternative views, to create a bookmark, to interact with or tweet the thing rather than simply contemplate it.[9]

Acting upon what we've just read, rather than stopping to meditate and think, is an impulse that we bring to reading books. I find it in my own reading patterns. I am quick to Tweet and slow to think. I am quick to Google and slow to ponder.

So ask yourself the next time you read: When you come across a provoking or perplexing portion of a book, what are you more likely to do: *react* or *think*? When you are tempted to react, stop, and simply think and meditate about what you are reading.

Ready Access to Information vs. Slowly Digested Life Wisdom

The third challenge gets to the heart of Socrates's concern. Valuable life wisdom flows out of meditation and deep thought.

It's easy to skim around for information online or to bounce from one fragmented detail to another. But the labor gets heavy when we determine to study a book for the purpose of gaining life wisdom. True learning and true wisdom are the fruit of long-term diligent study and meditation, benefits that we cannot get from books unless we are willing to slow our minds, mute distractions, and carefully think about what we are reading.

The skill to read a few books deeply for the purpose of gaining wisdom requires intentional and countercultural concentration. Of all the people surrounded by data in the information age, Christians should be especially protective of the time required to slowly meditate (Proverbs 4).

Skimming with the Head vs. Delighting with the Heart

Lest we put all the blame on the Internet, however, the hasty reading of books appears to be a problem that predates Google. Puritan Thomas Brooks (1608–1680) faced this problem in seventeenth-century England. Brooks wrote,

> Remember, it is not hasty reading, but serious meditating upon holy and heavenly truths, that makes them prove sweet and profitable to the soul. It is not the bee's touching of the flower that gathers honey, but her abiding for a time upon the flower that draws out the sweet. It is not he that reads most, but he that meditates most, that will prove the choicest, sweetest, wisest, and strongest Christian.[10]

Slow meditation on what we read is not only essential for gaining wisdom, it is also essential for experiencing delight.

In order to *feel* deeply about spiritual truths we must *think* deeply. And to *think* deeply we must *read* deeply. And to *read* deeply we must read *attentively*, not hastily. If we discipline ourselves to read attentively and to think deeply about our reading, we will position our souls to delight. But our souls cannot delight in what our minds merely skim.

I am convicted as I write this. It is easy to talk about these challenges impersonally. But the fact is that each of these four challenges has emerged in my book reading and to some degree continues to plague me. One way they became obvious to me was when I began reading books on an e-book reader.

Kindle and Me

I read books on a Kindle e-book reader for eighteen months. In those months I discovered that I could read faster and that I could read more easily on jet planes, at the park, and in bed. I could download new books instantly. Never before had books been more accessible, and never had one hundred books fit more comfortably in my hand. With all these books I found myself flipping between multiple titles at the same time, becoming quickly tired with one book and switching to another, more promising, book.

About a year into my friendship with Kindle I noticed that my online reading habits were creeping into my e-book reading habits. All my distracted fragmented browsing habits began appearing as I read books on my Kindle. I noticed:

- I was less discerning with the e-books I was reading.
- I was experiencing a persistent feeling of being rushed.
- I was finding it difficult to maintain sustained linear attention.
- I rarely meditated while reading an e-book.
- I reacted to what I was reading, rather than stopping to think and meditate.
- I found myself tempted to flip to a different book unless the book arrested my attention at all times.

- I found myself browsing and skimming books. (The Kindle alerts readers what sections of a book have been most commonly highlighted by other readers, and I was often simply skipping from one popular paragraph to another.)

You may be more disciplined that I am (actually, there's a good chance of it). But in my life I noticed several unhelpful reading patterns emerge. No matter how I tried, I could not reverse them.

After eighteen months I went Kindle-free, and I recommitted my life to printed books.

Book reading devices are here to stay. E-books are convenient for consumers, profitable for writers, and simple for publishers (no pulp, no binding, no shipping, no shelf space).

As e-book devices advance and include Internet browsing, search engines, social media, and e-mail, they will only increase the potential for distractions. The peripheral temptations that disrupt book reading will be unavoidable—in fact they will become *inseparable* from the book itself!

I'm not saying I will never use an e-book reader in the future. But for now, when I read, I set my phone aside, unplug from the Internet, grab a printed book from my shelf, find a pen, and take the time to stroll through long stretches of prose.

Driving Away Distractions

So is Google making us stupid? I'm not sure we should lay all the blame at the feet of Google, Twitter, Facebook, Kindle, or iPad. If we cannot read books, we can blame ourselves. I blame myself. It was my thoughtless online browsing patterns that eroded the concentration I needed to read books.

The point of this chapter is not to unplug you from the Internet. If you are like me you *need* the Internet, search engines, e-mail, and social media. I depend on the Internet to connect with friends, to communicate with colleagues, and even to find and buy good books!

The point of this chapter is pretty simple: as Christians, convinced of the importance of book reading, we must periodically gauge the effects of the Internet and social media upon our lives. The concentration and self-discipline required to read books requires years of practice to build and consistent exercise to maintain. If we are careless, this concentration and discipline will erode, and we will find ourselves in a losing battle—losing our patience with books and losing our delight in reading.

The skill and concentration needed to read books is worth fighting for.

12

Marginalia

The Fine Art of Defacing Books with Pencils, Pens, and Highlighters

I was raised in public libraries and public schools. And I am fairly certain this is why I have a deeply entrenched aversion to writing in books. This fear was planted deep in my subconscious by librarians and teachers who sought to protect their books from irreverent rascals like me.

For many of us growing up, writing in books was not only discouraged, it was punishable. It was treated as a heinous and premeditated act. Some of us have been to the scene of a bibliohomicide. In the school library a book is discovered that has been sliced by a pen. The librarians pull the book from circulation, open its front cover, and dramatically stamp it in red ink: "Mutilated Copy." For weeks scowling librarians check student IDs with suspicion. A bibliokiller is on the loose.

I'm being dramatic, but the antimarginalia bias in the schools is not fictional. In fact, I know one grown man so traumatized that he finds it hard to fill out crossword puzzles!

Yet the markings in a book's margins are the evidence of a thinking reader. We don't read to read; we read to think. "My own conviction is that fruitful study is primarily thinking, not reading," John Piper says. "My guess is that reading, which was meant to become a stimulus and guide to independent thinking, usually becomes a substitute for it. The evidence for this is how many books we read and how little we write down."[1]

I have outgrown my marginaliaphobia. Now I think writing in a book is a sign of a healthy and mature reader. I write in my books—with pens!—and I think you should, too. This chapter is my attempt to convince you.

Why I Write in My Books

By now you know why I prefer printed books—the kind of books that friends can borrow, that pens can mark, and that Post-it notes can decorate. When I buy these books—even expensive new books—I don't hesitate to hack at them with highlighters and pens of all colors. And here are ten reasons why.

1. I write in my books to claim them. Whenever I buy a book that will become a permanent addition to my library, I write my name on the inside cover. It's a claim of ownership. It is my way of saying that this book belongs to me, it has been added to my library, and it is a tool for me to use as I see best.

2. I write in my books to acknowledge their temporary value. In the first chapter of this book, we discovered that all literature can be separated into two major genres—Scripture, and all other books. As much as I love books and literature, the books in my library are not eternal. Every physical book I own is in the process of returning to dust—"For you are paper pulp and to paper pulp you shall return." I keep this in mind when I uncap a pen and begin scrawling my notes into the pages of a book. My books are not fragile museum pieces to archive behind a glass display; my books are well-worn hand tools—hammers, tin snips, measuring tapes, and vice grips—to help me remodel my brain.

3. I write in my books to highlight what I appreciate. I mark phrases, sentences, paragraphs, and pages that I think articulate a point very well. I call them gold. The gold nuggets could be paragraphs, sentences, or even just phrases that I don't want to forget. I mark them so they stand out. I'll explain more about how I mark these later in the chapter.

4. *I write in my books to trace the skeleton of the book.* The publisher often leaves the reader with spacious white margins. I fill those margins with my own notes as I trace the author's arguments. Often, after I have completed a chapter, I return to the first page of the chapter to jot down a simple summary. My goal is to make the skeletal structure of the chapter more clear and obvious as I progress, especially in nonfiction books.

5. *I write in my books to mark what is initially disagreeable.* Remember what we learned earlier: it's often best to read straight through a chapter without stopping. If it's a book that I am trying to read quickly, I mark questions in the margin with a small question mark that I can return to later. But on the first pass I simply mark sections that I want to reconsider.

6. *I write in my books to weave them into my library.* In my books I often add counterarguments from other books or cross-references from other authors. I like to stitch together what I read in one book with the rest of my library. Writing in the margin allows me to patch in cross-references to other books. When I return to a book, I will be prompted to return to a cluster of books, and to specific chapters and pages that are related to a particular theme. In this way I weave my library together in the margins.

7. *I write in my books to express emotion.* Healthy readers experience emotions as they read. They express joy, concern, or even anger at times. A balanced range of emotional responses to books is a sign that we are engaged readers. And the margins are a great place to vent anger or sing praises. The raw thoughts of a reader are best written in the margin. And this is what makes borrowing books from readers who write in their books so fun! Documenting these emotional responses is one reason why I hold a pen in my hand as I read. The emotions displayed in the reading experience *can* be captured. They *should* be captured. Those marginal notes are where the mind of the

author and the mind of the reader collide. I hope my kids will one day read over my notes and see my responses to a book.

8. I write in my books to capture thoughts. Pick a business book off my bookshelf, and you will see my notes clustered in the margins and the blank pages in the beginning and the end of the book. But you will not find much interaction with the author. Mostly I write thoughts that have bounced around my mind as I read. Reading focuses my mind. By focusing my attention in a book and by blocking out the distractions of life (which is a rare experience), I find that my thoughts become clearer. With a focused mind, thoughts and ideas will bubble up as I read. I use the blank pages to capture those thoughts—about life, my work projects, and my personal goals.

9. I write in my books to archive personal notes. As I interact with topics in the margins of books, my books become personal notebooks of recorded reflections. I could use a blank Moleskine notebook, but that's not as convenient. In the margins of a book my thoughts are directly tied to the original source. In her book *Marginalia: Readers Writing in Books*, H. J. Jackson makes this important point.

> Writing notes on the page takes less time than turning aside to a notebook and poses less of a threat to the reader's concentration. In the long term, it has potential benefits for both parties [the original note writer and the future note reader]. As long as the notes are permanently attached to the text, the text stands as a reminder of the source and a corrective check on the interpretation. Annotated books also constitute a ready-made filing and retrieval system. Readers know where to find their notes.[2]

Marginal notes provide a convenient storage system for your own reflections and a way to anchor your thoughts to the thoughts of the author.

10. I write in my books in order to have a conversation. Odd, I know, but true. Marginal notes are transcripts of a sometimes-disturbing internal dialogue. This conversation goes in three different directions. First, the reader can address the author: "Yes! Well said, Mr. _____!" Or, "What are you thinking?" Second, the reader can give himself a little pep talk: "This is important. Don't forget this point especially in light of the previous chapter." Third, these notes can be a conversation with future readers: "Don't listen to what Chesterton says about Calvin. What a nut!" This little conversation is almost always worth recording in the margins.

Let me zero in on a few of these topics and explain *how* I mark up my books.

What to Mark and How to Mark It

Most of my book scribbles accomplish one of three goals: to highlight what I appreciate, to trace the structure of the book, or to critique what I don't appreciate.

Highlights

The most intuitive reason to write in a book is to highlight a gem of truth you want to remember. In one sense, highlighting serves your future self. You make it easy to find important portions of a book in the future.

As I said earlier, I collect quotes like some people collect antiques. I love to sift through thousands of pages of books for truth, goodness, and beauty. By highlighting as I read, it's easy to return to them later when I enter the quotes into my database.

When I discover a quote, sometimes I highlight it (although highlighter ink will often fade over the years), or I underline it with a pen (for a brief quotation), or I run a vertical line down the outside margin of the page alongside the text (for paragraphs). I run a single vertical line for selections that are *very important* and a double vertical line for selections that are *critically important*. When I flip through a previously read book, these highlights should be the most obvious markings. I draw these lines thick and bold.

Structure and Development

Active readers watch how an author develops a particular point. Piper said it well: "Most of us are cursed with a penchant toward passive reading. We read the way people watch TV. We don't ask questions as we read. We don't ask: Why does this sentence follow that sentence? How does this paragraph relate to that one three pages earlier?

We don't ferret out the order of thought or ponder the meaning of terms."[3] Not asking such questions is a matter of failing to read with an active mind.

Publishers are especially generous with all the white space on the first page of a chapter. That space is perfect for tracking chapter development. There I can connect the small details of a chapter together into a visual linear progression. As I progress through the chapter, I jot little summary phrases on that first page and connect them with arrows to note the progress from one idea to another. This is especially helpful when I cannot complete a chapter in a single sitting.

If I were reading this chapter, I would jot some notes on page 147. It might look something like this: *writing in books encouraged* → *10 reasons to write in a book* → *how to write in books*. These little notes help me visualize the trajectory of a chapter.

Naturally, section headings are critical for following the progression of a chapter. But a number of books—especially old books—are comprised of long sentences and paragraphs smashed together tighter than the stones of Solomon's temple. In that case it's necessary to crowbar the text apart with my own section headings written in the margin. It helps me comprehend what I'm reading.

And those blank pages in the front and back of a book function as a personal notebook for all types of notes, quotes, and questions.

The back pages I use for topical references. Whenever I read a book on Christian living, I make a note in the back for every reference that connects the Christian life to the truths of the gospel. I'll scribble out this category (and many others) to create my own little index. In the back of my books you will likely find a list like this:

Gospel and sanctification: 12, 56, 120, 187, 220

This means that I have found helpful references to the connection between the gospel and living out the Christian life on five pages. This little discipline helps me track reoccurring themes of personal interest. Those particular themes are determined before I begin my reading, thanks to two practices we talked about earlier (structuring reading around specific priorities and writing out questions that I expect a book to answer).

Discernment

Active readers must not become cynics, but they must be critics. A reader with a pen in hand is ready to read critically. Open to new discoveries? Yes. But always wielding biblically-sharpened discernment. Identifying the lowlights in a book is my means of drawing attention to sections or arguments that:

- *Appear to be wrong.* On first read, if a statement strikes me as questionable, I mark it so I can return later.
- *Lack collaborative evidence, substance, and persuasion.* It is the author's job to convince me. Where I think the author fails, I note it.
- *Lack biblical support for the claim.* The most dangerous theological books are the ones that fail to adequately provide biblical support for its claims. Noting this lack of support is critical for the protection of my own soul.
- *Recycle points from earlier in the book.* Business books are infamous for repeating the same points over and over, for saying the same thing time and time again, for making the same point chapter by chapter, and trying to use different wording to disguise the repetition. I note these repetitions.

Try It Once

Says Piper: "If it's worth reading, it's worth writing in." I agree. And if it's worth reading seriously, I think it's worth buying and marking up. But of course, if you want to write in books, please buy them first. Very few librarians appreciate marginalia. Respect your librarians and don't write in library books.

How you decide to write in your books will be as unique to you as your thumbprint. Be simple and begin with a pen, or get creative and develop a multicolored, multisymbolic system. Or, if all this talk of book graffiti makes you uneasy, start with a pencil.

Take these suggestions into your own hands and modify them for your own reading goals. But do try this at least once.

If you find it hard to write in books, I'll meet you halfway. I give you permission to mutilate chapter 13 for practice.

Happy hacking!

13

Reading Together

Building Community One Book at a Time

Building houses is in my blood—and I have the scars to prove it.

Ever since I could walk, I could swing a hammer. I've pounded thousands of nails in my lifetime. And I have pounded my own fingernail a few times along the way. (Note: The pain of slamming the same thumb twice in the same day is a throbbing sting beyond all description.)

Eventually I graduated from a hammer to a pneumatic nail gun, but that didn't stop the pain or the blood. (Note: The pain of shooting a framing nail through two angled boards and then completely through the left ring finger is actually not as bad as you might assume.)

Long before I was trusted with a pneumatic nail gun, my father taught me the proper setting of a framing nail. The process isn't complicated. Your left hand holds the nail steady, and with your right hand you gently tap the head of the nail—just enough so the nail sinks into the surface of the board and can stand on its own. Once the nail is set, you move your left hand out of the impact zone and pound and sink the nail down with a few mighty swings. Or, if you miss hitting the nail head squarely, the nail glances off the head of the hammer and shoots across the room like a bullet.

Reading a book and hammering a box of framing nails are surprisingly similar acts. When you read, your eye scans back and forth across a page, information (nails) appear quickly before your eyes, and you have just enough time to tap those concepts into the surface of your memory. For most of us, quickly reading over content in a book is like setting a nail. It's a good start, but if that is where we leave it, it will not hold tight, and eventually it will loosen and fall out. The fallen nail is a forgotten detail.

One great way to sink details deep into our long-term memory is to read and discuss books with friends. There we can slow our minds, focus our thoughts, and learn from others.

God intended books to be read for the benefit of the community. Reading benefits the community in at least three settings: as we read Scripture corporately (and learn together as a church), as we read books privately (and share what we learn with others), and as we read books in community (and discuss what we learn with others).

Lector

Historically, the church has benefitted from reading in three ways.

First, for centuries God's people have gathered for the public reading of Scripture. In the Old Testament, God's people gathered to hear Ezra read the Bible for six hours (Neh. 8:1–8). In the New Testament, the apostle Paul exhorted pastor Timothy to read the Bible publicly to his church (1 Tim. 4:13). The New Testament is comprised of letters (or epistles) that were written for the purpose of being read. The book of Revelation is one lengthy example (it takes seventy minutes to read Revelation verbally, according to my iTunes audio Bible).

In the early church, the public reading of Scripture was done chiefly by the *lector* (Latin for "reader"). The lector was the official public reader, and it's a role that Revelation 1:3 seems to mention: "Blessed is *the one who reads aloud* the words of this prophecy. . . ."

This use of a public reader—a *lector*—was renewed during the Reformation. Even as more believers learned to read and began carrying their own Bibles, the use of lectors continued. Many churches today continue to use lectors, with a deacon or a member of the church who reads Scripture in the weekly service. The reading often coincides with the preacher's sermon text.

The public reading of Scripture is an ancient tradition rooted in biblical history and carried through church history. From the beginning, the identity and solidarity of the church has been marked by the act of public reading.

The Currency of Trade

Second, reading has benefitted the believing community because what Christians read privately is intended to benefit the church. The Bible commands us to teach one another: "Let the word of Christ dwell in you richly, teaching and admonishing one another in all wisdom . . ." (Col. 3:16). We read and study "the word of Christ" for personal benefit and also for the benefit of our family and friends and neighbors. This point is made well by Spurgeon.

> When you read a passage of Scripture, and have any enjoyment therein, go to your sick neighbor and tell them what God has said to you. If you meet an ignorant one when you know somewhat of the things of God, tell them to him. Nations are enriched by the interchanges of commerce, and so are Christians. We each have something that another has not, and he has something that we need. Let us trade together.[1]

God's people read for the benefit of community. What we learn by reading is the currency for our trade with others. We use our private reading as a means of blessing the body of Christ.

Reading Books Together

Third, books benefit the community when we gather to read books together. As people of the Book, we prioritize books and reading, and we naturally prize opportunities to gather to read together, especially theologically rich books.

Theology is especially suited for reading within the community of faith, because the community shares a personal stake in its promises. Marilynne Robinson says this beautifully:

Good theology is always a kind of giant and intricate poetry, like epic or saga. It is written for those who know the tale already, the urgent messages and the dying words, and who attend to its retelling with a special alertness, because the story has a claim on them and they on it. . . . Theology is written for the small community of those who would think of reading it. So it need not define freighted words like "faith" or "grace" but may instead reveal what they contain. To the degree that it does them any justice, its community of readers will say yes, enjoying the insight as their own and affirming it in that way.[2]

Theology books belong in community. Rick Ritchie agrees. In an article in *Modern Reformation*, he argues that Christians should read broadly from writers throughout church history—and they should read together. "Aside from a re-reading of the New Testament," he writes, "a reading of old Christian authors is probably the best way of challenging our own complacency with our understanding of the good Christian life."[3] Ritchie encourages Christians to read broadly, and to read broadly together. Reading broadly together brings encouragement and protection:

Reading broadly together will keep me from always being on a new crusade to the bewilderment of Christian friends. The Christian purpose of all of this reading is to glorify God. Reading alone may do this, but when we become passionate about an issue it is nice to have company. When we have seen things rightly, others can support us. When we have missed the mark, they can correct us. It is gratifying, however, when the new viewpoint which seemed so exciting to me is adopted by the others. When I make a new discovery it will often seem implausible for the simple fact that no one around me sees what I now see. If friends travel the same road, all is different.[4]

Reading books together with other Christian friends provides us with a place for collective discernment, and a place for spiritual illumination. And those are sweet moments!

Love to Read/Hate to Read

Sadly, many Christians don't read books. Why? I suppose there are many answers to this question. But primarily I think a lot of Christians have not journeyed far into book reading because they have not traveled this road with friends. What better introduction to the value of reading than through a brother or sister in Christ?

Maybe this is you. Is reading a daunting chore? I'd encourage you to find those in your church who love to read. Watch them. Learn from them. Catch their love of reading. Find others who will help you benefit from books, and you will eventually notice your own growing desire to read.

Or do you already love to read? That desire is God's gift to be shared with those around you. If you love to read, find someone who doesn't, grab two copies of a book, go sit in a coffee shop, and grow in grace together. This is one way God's gifts to introverted Christians blesses those in the local church.

We can bless others, and we can learn from others, as soon as we put away the idea that reading is a solitary exercise. It is not. At least not for Christians. As I will explain in the next chapter, my love for reading was ignited when I ran into a pastor who was willing to walk me through his library of books. All Christian readers have an opportunity to encourage other readers in the same way.

We fail to see God's plan for books if we view reading as nothing more than a discipline done in isolation and for nothing more than personal edification. So what can be done?

Start a Reading Group

Starting a reading group with a few friends is one great way to read books. And starting one is not difficult. Here are few suggestions.

Aim for small and informal. Your first reading group does not need to be large. In fact I would encourage you to start small with a group of two to five friends. Write a list of people to invite, select a book to read, create a general schedule (and especially a completion date), and then send out invitations. But do keep it relatively small. Sometimes reading groups get derailed because they are too large and too ambitious. Staying small allows for greater flexibility.

Choose your book wisely. In building a reading group around a particular book, take sufficient time to choose the book. Ask your pastor for recommendations. Reading groups are wonderfully flexible. You can read Scripture together in the form of a Bible study. You can read theology, Christian living, or devotional works together. You can even read Christian biographies, novels, poems, or even (on some occasions) non-Christian literature. I know of Christians in the business world who gather for coffee to discuss a new business book with an open Bible and an engaged Christian worldview. This flexible range of genres is possible because we bring with us a Christian worldview that we use to discern (see chap. 4). Whatever book you pick, make certain it's a book that is important enough to sustain the group's attention.

Or don't choose a book at all. Obviously most reading groups will be centered on one book, but that's not a requirement, and it's certainly not the only approach to a reading group. A friend of mine once started a reading group that simply gathered to benefit from what each group member was reading individually. A group like this can survive on a more flexible schedule. Perhaps the most famous example is The Inklings, a group started in the 1930s by a handful of friends living in Oxford, England (the two most famous being C. S. Lewis and J. R. R. Tolkien). They gathered to read selections from their own works and then to discuss them. The Inklings model is pretty simple: bring what occupies your mind and read it aloud. Stimulating the minds of others and generating conversation makes it possible to learn from one another.

Read verbally. Let's assume that your reading group is centered on one book (most likely this will be the case). In this setting, make it a point to read specific sections out loud together. You know how it is—life is busy and reading assignments get neglected, or even worse, rushed to the point that the reading makes no impression. Locate especially important paragraphs and pages, and in your meeting take time to read these excerpts aloud. Many of my most memorable reading group meetings featured lengthy sections of a book read verbally and slowly. Never underestimate the value and power of simply reading important passages together as a group.

Build up, don't exhaust. In my first few attempts at leading a reading group, my goal was to be exhaustive—and no doubt I was exhausting, too. The goal of a reading group is *not* to exhaust a book, discuss every important point, or cover every chapter equally. The goal is to use our books as scaffolding so that our discussions build up one another. This distinguishes book reading in the Christian community from Oprah's book club. Our goal is not to finish a book, or merely to talk about a book, but to use our books to grow Christlike character (Rom. 8:29; Eph. 4:11–13; Col. 3:5–11; 2 Cor. 3:18).

Our books are a means to this end, and our reading groups position us to teach one another, to learn from one another, to pray for one another, to admonish one another, to build up one another, and to praise God together. Our books are a means to fellowship and edification. If this is happening, don't be troubled by how little of the book is covered in detail.

Agree to disagree (with the author). Learning from an author you all agree with is a wonderful thing. But sometimes you will all disagree with the author. That's okay—the group has not failed. Disagreements can become rich and rewarding discussions in themselves, because it suggests that the group is engaged, thinking, and discerning! Group leaders need to be prepared for disagreements. Even the most perfect or imperfect literature will prove disagreeable at times. The amount of unified disagreement with an author has often caught me off guard. But I have come to cherish these opportunities. Reading groups have helped shape my discernment in ways few other contexts can provide. And no other setting has more convinced me that Scripture is the only book that is perfect, sufficient, eternal, and transcendent.

Commit to mutual humility. Ultimately, reading groups that seek to pursue Christlikeness together will succeed only if the men and women who populate those groups are humble. Reading books for personal growth brings a holy equality. The experienced Christian and the new believer can walk through many of the same books on the Christian life together and mutually benefit because they are each a sinner in need of a Savior and in need of each other.

But if your reading group is a stage for a few to show off, the discussion will get derailed, and those who are timid will be discouraged and marginalized. Rather than edifying, the group will breed pride, envy, and grumbling.

The tenor of the group is drastically altered by humility. In a humble group there is no superior wrath-deserving sinner over another; there are only sinners seeking grace together, in search of ways to serve one another.

From the outset of the reading group, make this point clear. Ask others to commit their hearts to involvement in this group with humble and teachable hearts, where each member shows up to the meetings out of honor for one another and selfless love, postured to serve and to learn from the group.

Calvin and Friends

At the same time I began writing this book, I began meeting with three friends to read John Calvin's thick theology *The Institutes of the Christian Religion*. I tossed together a loose schedule, and we met in my basement every couple of weeks to discuss fifty pages of reading and to read sections out loud. (*The Institutes*, when read verbally, is a strikingly beautiful work.)

Meeting together with friends to "talk theology" invigorated my soul and built my faith. In those meetings we delighted in God's sovereignty, worshiped Jesus for his death on the cross and resurrection from the grave, and delighted in our union with Christ and all the saving benefits we receive in him. My friends are humble and wise, and I have learned a lot from them. They have shaped me by their piety and wisdom. They are friends on the same road, and they have traded with me—giving me far more than I have given them.

I love that God designed books and reading for the purpose of our mutual edification.

Conclusion

Literacy and good books provide us with the nails; disciplined reading sets those nails; and our community helps to sink a few of those carefully chosen nails firmly in our minds and hearts.

If you're like me, you know only a few select ideas will be sunk deeply into your long-term memory. That's the reality of reading books. Most nails are set, but never sunk. A good reading group will determine which of the nails to drive tight and which nails to leave hanging. But choose carefully. It's the ideas and passages from books that are discussed most carefully with friends that are sunk the furthest into the mind, and those sunk the furthest are the ones you will carry the longest. Those are the truths that remain on the tongue when you trade with other needy sinners in your life.

While reading is mostly a solitary task—and a very important one—comprehension is a community project. I am convinced that we forget so much of what we read not because we are *poor* readers, rather, I believe we forget so much of what we read because we are *selfish* readers. And we all suffer because of it.

14

Raising Readers

*How Parents and Pastors Can Ignite in Others
a Love for Book Reading*

As a child reads, so a child becomes. Dozens of educational studies show how books impact the trajectory of a child's life. A child who is trained to read well is more likely to excel educationally and professionally.

Similarly, historical theology shows how God has protected and built the church through the arrival of the right books at the right time.

In the home and in the church, books are critically important tools.

This chapter will equip two groups that are positioned to encourage reading in the lives of others—parents and pastors. It will help parents and pastors think creatively about how they can ignite in others a desire to read books.

We start with parents.

Tips for Parents
Our children are flooded daily with electronic media and visual simulation. Parents may be slinging sandbags in response, but the

tidal wave of electronic media is winning. According to a 2010 study, the average child (ages eight to eighteen) invests more than seven hours per day watching TV, playing video games, listening to music, or browsing the Internet.[1] A *New York Times* article stated the findings bluntly: "The average young American now spends practically every waking minute—except for the time in school—using a smartphone, computer, television or other electronic device."[2] And that's bad news for books.

So how can parents plug the holes in this cultural flood and raise children who love to read? The answer is to make books *prominent* and reading *delightful*. Here are some suggestions.

1. *Fill your home with books*. Many of history's most prolific readers, writers, and leaders were raised in homes stuffed with books. C. S. Lewis said that on a rainy day he could pull a random book off his family's bookshelf and know he had never read it. And C. H. Spurgeon had an open invitation to his grandfather's library of seventeenth-century Puritan theology books. As early as seven years old, Charles soaked for hours in that library, while the books shaped his mind, informed his soul, and prepared him for the 3,500-plus sermons he would preach in his ministry! Without great books we don't have great preachers, or great writers, or great leaders.

Fill your home with a library of books. To save paper (or money), go to the library. The point is to make books visible and prominent, so your children will see books as worthwhile and enjoyable.

2. *Read to your kids*. Perhaps the best way to prioritize book reading is to read to your children. This provides time for parents and children to bond, and it offers the parent an opportunity to help model reading.

In his famous book on reading, Mortimer Adler draws an important distinction between *aided* and *unaided* discovery. We all begin as readers who require *aided discovery*, that is, initially we need parents, pastors, classrooms, and teachers to help us to learn from books. Someone must help us see truth, goodness, and beauty in our books. But over time, as we develop literary skills, we begin to make *unaided discoveries* on our own. Parents who read to their children and who pause and reflect on what they read are helping children make *aided discoveries*. This practice is a way to train children to later make *unaided discoveries* on their own.

Determining the best time to read together can be tricky. Reading at the end of a long and busy day can be difficult, and it's at bedtime that my wife and I are more likely to nod off while reading a book to our children (not an impression that encourages literacy!). So instead of bedtime reading we sometimes read for twenty minutes after dinner. Apparently I scarf my food much faster than my kids nibble theirs, leaving me enough time to read a short chapter or story as they finish. Think creatively, experiment with different times, and mix up the settings to determine what works best for your family. But do read together, and read together often.

3. *Don't stop reading to your kids.* Christians appreciate the value of a life-long commitment to reading. Parents should continue to read verbally to their children as they grow older.

In his book, *The Read-Aloud Handbook,* Jim Trelease makes a compelling argument for why parents must continue reading to teenage children. As they mature, the distractions of life become louder and the academic pressures become stronger. He argues that high dropout rates among college freshmen can be traced back to a lack of literacy skills in the home, and ultimately to parents who wrongly assumed that teenagers are too old to hear books read aloud. Not so, he argues. Parents should read aloud to their children from birth until college, the point in their lives when literacy plays the most important role in their educational success.

4. *Read your books in front of your kids.* Young children prize what they see their parents prize. Over the months that I have written this book, my small children frequently come sit down next to me at a table with a stack of blank paper. They tell me they intend to write a book, too.

In the same way, reading a book in front of your kids will promote literacy. Do both, of course—read your books in front of them, and read their books to them—but let your kids see you reading. Let them see the stack of books that you are working on, and let them see that reading books is a high priority in your own life.

Depending on your job and schedule, your serious reading may be done when the kids are not around: early in the morning, at your office desk, or late at night. That means it's more likely they will see you doing "light reading" or no reading at all. Be intentional about also doing some "heavy reading" in the presence of your children. Let it be obvious to them that books are cherished in your own life.

5. *Teach young children to read.* Learning to walk is natural; learning to read is unnatural. Learning to read is like learning to play a piano—it will not happen without intention, focus, and discipline. Every child will learn to read at a different pace, but try to teach your children to read early.

Of course, training our little kids to read will require our time. It will try our patience, and it will test the limits of our perseverance. But that's true of all our greatest priorities in life.

As you train them in the basics of reading, find ways to motivate your children. We have motivated our children by offering to buy them brand new books when they can begin to read simple sentences. And we encourage them by offering to take them on "dates" to the local library. Find strategic ways to cheer them on as they learn to read.

6. *Push entertainment into the background.* On average, girls are better readers than boys. Multiple literacy studies, done in countries around the world, have proven this. It's especially hard to persuade boys of the joys of reading books. This is true for two reasons. First, there is an absence of masculine reading models in a young boy's life. Dads who don't read—and there are a lot of them—will rarely raise boys who read. Second, there is a pervasive influence of video games in a boy's life.

In his article "How to Raise Boys Who Read," Thomas Spence writes, "The secret to raising boys who read, I submit, is pretty simple—keep electronic media, especially video games and recreational Internet, under control (that is to say, almost completely absent). Then fill your shelves with good books."[3]

It is not impossible to enjoy reading and entertainment, but your priorities must be settled first. In our home, reading is the priority over video games and television and movies. This is modeled in how we talk about books and how we limit electronic media.

To confront the flood of digital media, parents must sometimes throw sandbags to keep a boundary around our children where a love for reading can safely develop.

7. Listen to audio books in the car. Over the years we have logged many miles on the road for family vacations. We have grown to anticipate these road trips and the opportunity they present for the entire family to enjoy audio books. Before we leave on a lengthy car trip, we borrow CDs from the library or download audio books online. By the time we pull out of the driveway, we are well stocked. These books inform, entertain, and always help cultivate our children's imaginations.

8. Hunt for the best books. Book guides to the best in children's literature are readily available. Take time to plan books by season, by personal interest, and even by school studies. Talk with other parents in your church to find reliable recommendations. And if a book does not seem to be igniting a desire to read in your child, find a different book. Just because the book has a bronze medallion on the front cover doesn't mean it will make a good read-aloud book, nor does it mean it will capture your child's attention.

9. Anticipate new books. My wife and I seek to connect our children's reading interest with specific authors. Once we discover an author that our child really enjoys, we watch local book signings and new book releases. We don't stand in line at midnight waiting for the book to go on sale, but we do anticipate release dates and look forward to forthcoming books. This is a little practice that builds anticipation in our children for books and helps them appreciate the value of good books and gifted authors.

10. Celebrate the classics. This year we celebrated Hobbit Day (September 22) as a family in honor of the birthdays of Bilbo and Frodo Baggins, two characters in J. R. R. Tolkien's classic epic The Lord of the Rings. The kids dressed in hobbit costumes, we cooked rabbit stew, we walked barefoot, and after dinner (our sixth hobbit-like meal of the day!) we read together the story of the hobbit's birthday celebration. Find ways to get significant dates from your favorite books, and the birthdays of your favorite authors, into your calendar so you can celebrate.

11. Cultivate your child's moral imagination. In chapter 6 I sought to persuade you to cultivate your imagination. In the same way, imaginative literature like myth and fantasy is not only permissible for children, but it provides us with an opportunity to cultivate the moral imagination of our children. Our family has been blessed by the moral lessons in C. S. Lewis's Chronicles of Narnia. The rich spiritual and moral lessons in these books make rereading them a priority in our home. Currently we are cultivating the moral imagination through a collection of fictional stories based on the lessons taken from selected Proverbs (Peter Leithart's *Wise Words: Family Stories That Bring the Proverbs to Life*).

Find books that picture moral lessons in the imagination, and savor those books with your children.

12. Help interpret worldviews as you read to your children. Reading vocally to your kids allows you to engage the book with a Christian worldview. Children's fictional books especially provide us with something of a "worldview simulator" where we can apply the biblical worldview to the storyline and to the lives of the characters.

Reading literature together allows parents to read about sin and evil and goodness and beauty—and to pause and help the child interpret those realities in light of Scripture (see chap. 4). In this way books (even non-Christian fiction) provide parents with a way to train and prepare our children to confront real-life situations, sinful attitudes, and worldly thinking. Ultimately we can use books to show our children where a biblical worldview and real life connect or clash.

13. Read your favorite excerpts to your children. Sometimes we can invite our children to experience what we are reading. I try to read favorite sections of literature with my children. My kids are not ready to read *The Odyssey* and *Beowulf,* but there are sections that I bring to the dinner table to read to them. I find that many of the imaginative books that I enjoy are either too long or too deep for my children to grasp. My goal is to locate a particular passage I enjoy and share it with my kids. For my boys this means reading an excerpt of the hero engaged in battle. For my daughter, this means finding the princess in peril. This simple exercise shows my children a love of reading, and it serves them a sweet dessert of prose.

14. Invite your children to read to the family. My oldest son (nine) devours books by the dozen. He is making his own unaided discoveries now, but we encourage him to share with us what he is reading. I will buy him as many books as he can read, so long as he agrees to mark his five favorite pages in each book, bring those marked pages to the dinner table, explain the context, and read them to the family. This practice models a love of reading for his younger brother and sister. It also helps reveal our son's heart to us, because we get a glimpse into what themes and concepts are most likely to capture his attention.

15. Challenge your children to improve books. When the time is appropriate, encourage your kids to disagree with a book. Ask them questions. What would you change about the book? How would you have written it? Do you have a better ending? Encourage your children to improve the book, to deconstruct the book, and to reconstruct it in a better way. These questions invite children to interact critically with books—a vital skill for all book readers!

16. Most importantly, read the Bible together as a family. Books are a big part of our home, but the Bible is the supreme Book. Parents model the primacy of Scripture by reading the Bible together as a family on a regular basis. Closed Bibles will not convince our children of the value of the Bible. We must open our Bible and read together. Currently we read Scripture together as a family after breakfast each morning.

But there are other important reasons for why we read Scripture. The Bible can be (and should be) at the center of our literacy. Pastor and father of three, Douglas Wilson, writes,

> Because we are people of the *Word*, it has been the most natural thing in the world for us to be people of *words*. Because we want our children to have access to the Word of God, we make a special point of teaching them all how to read. But of course, once we have opened up the Scriptures for them, they go on to read (and write) many other things. The Scriptures are the center, not the periphery. Because we know the centrality of the Word, we can enjoy many

other kinds of literature—from haiku to The Lord of the Rings—throughout the rest of our lives. But when the centrality of Scripture is lost, then uninspired letters cannot avoid disintegration.[4]

Don't miss this point. The Bible holds together the center of literacy in the lives of our children. By reading the Bible together, we are building for them the center that can hold all of their reading and writing together.

So those are a few practices that have helped encourage our children to treasure books. Each of these ideas was used at some point in our home, but not necessarily all at once. So please don't weary yourself trying to do all these things. Choose a few of the ideas—or just one—and work them into your home. Do what it takes to ignite in the green branches of your children a burning love of reading.

Tips for Pastors

When I became a new believer, I met a pastor who loved books. And that pastor lit under my reading list a desire to read that has never diminished. I can recall in vivid detail one fall cookout on the church's back lawn. At some point as the celebration began winding down, my pastor called me aside and we bailed from the party to his office library to talk books. Jumping from title to topic, pulling books and reading excerpts, he narrated the importance and value of great books. This "biblioshepherding" early in my Christian life fueled my reading appetite and directed my reading list.

Men like my pastor are important resources because there are young men who want to read, but who need direction. So how can pastors encourage reading? Here is a list of suggestions.

1. *Make opportunities to talk books.* Encouraging men to read is as simple as getting them into your own library. Show them the books that have helped you. Explain books, show them how you have organized them, and even lend some. Pastors can assume that a large portion of the men in their church rarely observed their dads reading books, and as a result they are intimidated and often overwhelmed in a library. They need a mentor. Pastor, you

can be that testimony, you can be that example, you can be that life-changing mentor.

2. *Illustrate sermon points with classic literature.* Pastors can feel an enormous pressure to quote and illustrate sermons from the latest "reality" TV shows, popular movies, contemporary music, and YouTube videos. Why not pull illustrations from classic literature? To illustrate a sermon, look to the stories by Dostoevsky, Tolstoy, or Shakespeare. Classic literature connects with people and provides a largely untapped storehouse of soul-stirring sermon illustrations.

3. *Pepper your sermon with direct quotes from Christian living books.* Many of the most profound excerpts from books that have shaped my own heart were excerpts carefully chosen and read verbally in a sermon. Pastors that can select and share excerpts from books not only model the value of reading and encourage literacy, they make subtle book recommendations based on specific needs in the local church.

4. *Lead a book discussion group.* Leading discussion groups is not easy, but it can be a rewarding role for a pastor. And great books are available on almost every topic and for every group. A pastor can lead a teen group through fictional allegory (like *The Pilgrim's Progress* by John Bunyan), he can lead a group of business readers through a book on glorifying God in the workplace (like *Luther on Vocation* by Gustaf Wingren), he can lead a group of men in a discussion on theology (like *Knowing God* by J. I. Packer), or he can lead his church in a discussion of a novel that stirs spiritual reflection (like *The Screwtape Letters* by C. S. Lewis). Reading groups led by pastors are especially helpful in identifying and training young leaders within the church.

5. *Start a church library or book table.* Make good books easily available to your people. There's no need to have a huge library or bookstore. Pick five to ten titles and quote from them or mention them at some point in your announcements or preaching. By making the books visible on Sunday, you make a bold statement about what the church believes theologically, and you make a bold statement about the importance of reading for Christians.

6. *Maintain a list of recommended books on your church website.* Especially if you don't have the funds to maintain a church bookstore, maintain a recommended reading list on the church website or blog. Don't load it with all the books you read in seminary. Keep the titles diverse, including theology and Christian living, even literature and poetry. Keep the list to the "best of the best" and be sure to freshen it with new titles as you discover them.

7. *Suggest books regularly as part of a book-of-the-month feature.* Consider recommending a new book each month. Hold the book up, explain the value of the book in your own life, and preview how others will benefit from reading it. Ensure that copies are available when you make the announcement.

8. *Recommend chapters of books.* Very often pastors will be asked for recommendations on a particular topic of the Christian life. C. J. Mahaney has found it helpful to recommend chapters from a book rather than an entire book. With this practice, he can avoid intimidating nonreaders, and he can use the chapter as a specific tool to address a specific need in someone's life. This is especially helpful when working with younger Christians who would be overwhelmed by an entire book on theology or Christian living. Consider each chapter that you read in a Christian living book as an individual tool for your pastoral use.

9. *Answer theological questions with pages from books.* Inevitably people in your church will raise theological questions. When they do, find the answers in theological books, photocopy the pages, highlight the relevant material, and give it to them to read. This act will model the relevance of reading, and it's a small way to say to them that the important questions in life are addressed in the pages of books. It reveals how relevant books are to real life.

10. *Give books as gifts.* For visitors, for members, for new parents, for whatever reason, find opportunities to gift books in your church. Set aside funds in the church budget for this. Books are meaningful gifts, they can serve a strategic function in the life of the reader, and they invite others in the church to experience the delights of reading.

Conclusion

I suspect most avid book readers have mentors who influenced them. God has positioned parents and pastors to model a love of book reading to their children and to their flocks. Making books appealing in this culture is especially difficult, but igniting a love of reading in others is a high calling worthy of our time, planning, and foresight.

15

Happily Ever After

Five Marks of a Healthy Book Reader

Becoming a great reader is no accident. Throughout this book we have addressed some of the most common challenges to reading. In this final chapter I offer five characteristics of a mature reader. These are five goals I aim at in my own life, and they are goals that I constantly work to apply.

1. Mature readers prize wisdom.
2. Mature readers cherish old books.
3. Mature readers keep literature in its place.
4. Mature readers avoid making books into idols.
5. Mature readers cling to the Savior.

Mature Readers Prize Wisdom

Not all books are safe, and not all reading habits are healthy.

The proliferation of published books can leave a reader exhausted, wearied, and burdened. Long before ink was spread over typeset letters in Gutenberg, Solomon anticipated this rapid expansion of book publishing when he wrote: "Of making many books there is no end, and much study is a weariness of the flesh" (Eccles. 12:12).

A title search for "Ecclesiastes" at Amazon.com lists 1,800 books. Solomon would see the irony in that. His warning has never been more necessary than in our culture today, where high-speed presses crank out thousands of new books every hour.

But life is more than books. With all the new books being published—and all the old books still available—we must be careful to avoid over studying. For many of you, this will not be a problem. The risk is for those who want to read every book that looks interesting. If this is you, you will run the risk of book fatigue. You will exhaust yourself, Solomon says. For one's life does not consist in the abundance of books.

Readers who weary themselves by excessively reading books get an "F" from Professor Solomon in Reading 101. Why? Book-induced exhaustion reveals a bigger failure, a negligence of wisdom.[1] A wide gap separates a reader who simply *consumes books* from a reader who diligently *seeks wisdom*. Book consumers view books as "things to get read." Wisdom seekers view books as fuel for slow and deliberate meditation.

The differences between the two can be seen in how they treat books. A book consumer will read a great book and then treat it like "a burnt-out match, an old railway ticket, or yesterday's paper," wrote C. S. Lewis.[2] On the other hand, a wisdom seeker will read a great book, savor it, and reread it in the future. Readers who cherish wisdom will reread great books five or ten or even twenty times.

The point is that if you cannot read a lot of books, don't sweat it. Find a few books, read them well, cherish the wisdom they provide, and apply that wisdom to your life. Then repeat. Always beware of an approach to reading books that fails to delight in wisdom. The consumer approach to reading is exhausting and dangerous to your health.

Prize the wisdom that you discover in books.

Mature Readers Cherish Old Books

Watch closely, and you'll notice that the publishing world is in a state of constant change. Books are changing in their appearance and in their readability. Many of the changes are good improvements. Take book length for example. Books are getting shorter, and excessively long sentences are being cut down into more manageable sizes. Chapters are shorter. Sentences are shorter. Authors are more to the point. In many ways these changes are improvements.

However, these changes in book publishing have a drawback: they accelerate the aging of old books. Like never before, old books are growing really old, really fast. Books from the 1980s already seem old to me. Books from the 1680s sometimes appear to be written in a foreign language—the words and concepts and idioms are so foreign and hard to understand. And Shakespeare? That's like trying to read a foreign language in the fog, at night, without my glasses on!

Yet, as Christians who treasure an ancient book (the Bible), we esteem old books. And perhaps nobody has better articulated the value of old books than C. S. Lewis in his introduction to the ancient classic, *On the Incarnation*, written by Athanasius (ca. AD 297–373). In the introduction, which was written in 1944, Lewis argues that old books are important for three reasons.

First, old books are the best way to understand people and thoughts and debates from the past. Rather than trying to swim in the complex secondary literature that seeks to interpret past controversy, Lewis argues that readers may actually find it easier to simply read the old books themselves.

Second, Lewis argues that old books are trusted books. They have been authenticated through the ages. A new book is still on trial, and its long-term value is yet to be decided. Old classics survive because they have been verified as classics.

Third, Lewis argues that old books freshen our minds from the stale air that settles in contemporary literature. They may be old books, but they are fresh words. Old books bring us fresh controversy, fresh voices, and fresh arguments. Here Lewis delivers his most famous words on the importance of old books:

> The only palliative is to keep the clean sea breeze of the centuries blowing through our minds, and this can be done only by reading old books. Not, of course, that there is any magic about the past.

People were no cleverer then than they are now; they made as many mistakes as we. But not the *same* mistakes. They will not flatter us in the errors we are already committing; and their own errors, being now open and palpable, will not endanger us. Two heads are better than one, not because either is infallible, but because they are unlikely to go wrong in the same direction.[3]

As I write this chapter, I sit in the second floor of a house that overlooks Cape Cod and the Atlantic Ocean. The sea breeze on this sunny, sixty-degree day is flowing in the open windows, refreshing me as I work. Old books are like that sea breeze, Lewis writes. The ideas and convictions and warnings of previous centuries blow through our lives and freshen our perspectives. (By the way, notice Lewis's intended paradox? Old books = fresh air. New books = stale air.)

Reading old books sure sounds nice, but in reality contemporary books are easier to read (and typically shorter, too). So where do we begin?

One helpful model comes from the life of Dr. Mark Dever, senior pastor of Capitol Hill Baptist Church in Washington, DC. Dever uses an annual reading schedule to ensure that the clean sea breeze is blowing in his mind throughout the year. He selects specific authors in history, what he calls his "canon of theologians." Each month he focuses on a specific author. For example, in March, Dever reads books by (and about) German Reformer Martin Luther. His reading has included Roland Bainton's biography *Here I Stand: A Life of Martin Luther*, Luther's *95 Theses*, and Luther's *The Bondage of the Will*.

Dever's annual reading schedule is structured chronologically, and it looks something like this:

- January: early church patristic writings (first through third centuries)
- February: Augustine (354–430)
- March: Martin Luther (1483–1546)
- April: John Calvin (1509–1564)
- May: Richard Sibbes (1577–1635)
- June: John Owen (1616–1683) and John Bunyan (1628–1688)

- July: Jonathan Edwards (1703–1758)
- August: C. H. Spurgeon (1834–1892)
- September: B. B. Warfield (1851–1921)
- October: Martyn Lloyd-Jones (1899–1981)
- November: C. S. Lewis (1898–1963) and Carl F. H. Henry (1913–2003)
- December: Contemporary authors

This list may frighten you, but I give it only as an example. You can modify it and insert your own list of authors. The strength of this model is its priority on old books. With this list Dever is able to freshen his mind throughout the year with old books by some of the greatest authors in church history.

Consider starting with Athanasius's book *On the Incarnation*, which was originally published in AD 318. Be sure to grab the version that includes Lewis's introduction. The book is old, but it's also simple and concise. Writes Lewis, "Only a master mind could, in the fourth century, have written so deeply on such a subject with such classical simplicity."[4] Athanasius's book is one example of just how readable old books—even ancient books!—can be for modern readers.

Maturing readers will learn to read old books—and to cherish them. And for a reader naturally drawn to the "new releases" at the bookstore, this is a lesson I preach to myself frequently.

Mature Readers Keep Literature in Its Place

Throughout this book I have encouraged you to value great literature. There are many classic books by both Christian and non-Christian authors. I think we should treasure great books wherever we find them. But we do not prize literature to the same extent that many non-Christian readers do. As Christians, the supremacy of Scripture curbs our appraisal of everything else we read and cautions us from overvaluing literature. Again, Lewis is instructive:

> The Christian will take literature a little less seriously than the cultured Pagan: he will feel less uneasy with a purely hedonistic standard for at least many kinds of work. *The unbeliever is always*

apt to make a kind of religion of his aesthetic experiences; he feels ethically irresponsible, perhaps, but he braces his strength to receive responsibilities of another kind which seem to the Christian quite illusory. He has to be "creative"; he has to obey a mystical amoral law called his artistic conscience; and he commonly wishes to maintain his superiority to the great mass of mankind who turn to books for mere recreation. *But the Christian knows from the outset that the salvation of a single soul is more important than the production or preservation of all the epics and tragedies in the world.* . . . The real frivolity, the solemn vacuity, is all with those who make literature a self-existent thing to be valued for its own sake.[5]

As Christians we cannot make literature our religion. We do not value literature for itself. We do not worship classics. We treasure values and priorities that far exceed the sum worth of the greatest library. Our end is not literature, no matter how true, good, and beautiful it is. Our end is God, the One from whom all truth, goodness, and beauty originates and finds its perfection.

Beauty originates in God, but beautiful literature makes for a puny, lousy god. Rather, we seek God, the gospel of his Son, and the salvation of souls. We are willing to sacrifice the time that we could use to read literature in order to serve our neighbors, pray for one another, fellowship with believers, and serve in our churches. We may not study literature as deeply as the world because we treasure souls seriously.

Christian readers will learn to keep literature in its proper place, and it's a lesson I am still learning.

Mature Readers Avoid Making Books into Idols

Our evaluation of literature is measured because we draw our ultimate delight in God. If we ask our personal library of books to fill our lives with ultimate joy, those books will fail, every time.

This was a lesson learned by John Newton, the eighteenth-century captain of a slave-trading ship turned preacher, writer, and abolitionist. In 1779 Newton published a three-volume collection of hymns titled *Olney Hymns*. It contains 348 hymns, mostly written by Newton, and it includes the famous hymn *Amazing Grace*. Upon hearing of the set's completion, Newton's friend John Ryland Jr. wrote a letter requesting a free copy. Newton sent along a set of the books but heralded their arrival with this preparatory letter:

> The hymn books will be with you soon, how soon I know not. Your hungry curiosity will not be long in appeasing. When you have read the preface, twirled over the pages, run your eye down the tables of contents, and have the book by you, you will feel much as you do about any other book that has been lying by you seven years. At least I have often found it so (but perhaps your heart is not just like mine). I have longed for a book, counted the hours till it came, anticipated a thousand things about it, flew to it at first sight with eagerness as a hawk at its prey; and in a little time it has been as quiet, as if placed upon the upper shelf in a bookseller's shop.[6]

My heart is just like Newton's. I order books online and track the status of the shipment. I wait eagerly for a box of books to arrive on my doorstep. As soon as the box arrives, I tear into it, pull out the books, investigate their condition, and begin twirling the pages in my fingers. This is a wonderful experience. But those new books lose their luster at around page 30.

When it comes to getting new books I may be the most spoiled man in the world, or at least that's what my wife and children say. Books arrive at my house far faster than I can read them. Everyday my heart desires new books. So what drives this desire? Is it a longing to humbly learn and grow? Or is it an idolatrous yearning to have more new things?

Books are great tools, but they are disappointing gods. And once books become idols, those idols will leave us deeply unsatisfied.

So I frequently I ask myself: Am I drawn to new books simply because I am drawn to new things? Or am I drawn to new books because I want to experience the truth, goodness, and beauty of the Giver?

Mature Readers Cling to the Savior

As you can see, I am an ambitious reader. And it's not uncommon for me to buy theology books that turn out to be too deep for my shallow brain. After opening the cover, it becomes clear that while the book in my hands may be in front of my face, the content on the pages is intellectually over my head, and I am drowning in a sea of complications and confusions.

No matter how hard I try, the further along into the book I travel, the deeper I sink into confusion and hopelessness. This is an awful experience.

This experience (and especially if the book is theological in nature) results in making me feel like a nitwit, even maybe less spiritual than my friends. Discouragement soon follows.

So how do we respond to books that clearly expose our intellectual limitations? Charles Spurgeon was aware of this temptation and confronted it head-on in his church:

> A few have I known who are troubled with doubts and fears because they do not understand as much as they would like to. They cannot read books of divinity [theology]; or, if they do read them, they get lost in a maze of difficult theological terms. They cannot reconcile certain truths. But this is no ground for fear, for the gospel is so simple that it is adapted even for those who are all but idiots. . . .

That is candid, but reassuringly true. The gospel is suited for simple folks (like me). Spurgeon continued:

> Think not, dear friend, that ignorance can push you out of the family of God. Little children cannot read Greek and Latin, but they can say, "Abba, Father," and that is all they need to say. If you cannot read books of deep theological lore, yet, if Jesus Christ be thine—if you are trusting in him—even the imperfect knowledge that you have of him proves that you are his, and he will never leave you, nor forsake you.[7]

Spurgeon *is not* encouraging Christians to avoid reading theology books. And Spurgeon *is not* encouraging us to give up when we face difficult words or abstract concepts in books. We need challenging books to grow.[8] But Spurgeon *is* reminding us that our confidence before God can only be in Jesus—not in how smart we are, not in how many theology books we read, not in how we order our reading priorities, not in how inefficiently we use our reading time. Childlike faith in the gospel is an unsinkable buoy when we find ourselves drowning in the details of a book that is over our head.

This is a fitting place to end our journey together.

Regardless of how many books we read, we cling to the old rugged cross. When books overwhelm us, and our intellectual limitations discourage us, we recall the gospel. In the good news of Jesus Christ, overwhelmed readers find peace, and joy, and the courage to keep reading.

In this place we are reminded of the Christian book reader's motto: "In your light do we see light" (Ps. 36:9). We are humbled, but we are encouraged. We grab a new book and we press on, not as slaves bound to a chore, but as liberated sinners who read to delight in the gifts of our God. We press on, reading and thanking God for the light we do see in books, and for his illuminating grace that lights our way.

Acknowledgments

"In an abundance of counselors there is safety" (Prov. 11:14). For me the abundance of counselors are my editors. The Lord has surrounded me with wise, humble, and gifted friends who pitched in to help make this book more interesting, more readable, and certainly more accurate.

Justin Taylor, my creative friend who initiated this book, handed it to me, and shepherded the book along. Without Justin there would be no book.

Drs. Leland Ryken, Gene Fant, Stephen Dempster, and Carl Trueman, a team of scholars, read portions of the book and sharpened the content and style.

C. J. Mahaney, my friend, my editor, my travel cohort, and my boss, has generously encouraged me and made my writing retreats possible.

Jon Vickery, a scholar, a clear thinker, and a friend, offered his help throughout the entire project. This book is much sharper as a result. I am indebted to his edits, suggestions, prayers, and friendship.

Special thanks to the team at Crossway: to Josh Dennis and the creative team for providing a brilliant cover image; to Tara Davis and the editorial team for their savvy copyedits; and to James Kinnard and his marketing team for their enthusiasm and encouragement.

Many other friends kindly agreed to read and edit the manuscript including Jon Smith, Mark Fedeli, Josh Deckard, Andrew Mahr, Carolyn McCulley, and Marylynne Tosyali.

Patrick Abendroth and Rick Gamache are the two pastors God used significantly to encourage my own literacy. When I speak of the pastor's ability to encourage Christians to read, these are two faithful examples have deeply impacted my own life.

Nora enables my bibliomania.

My dad, a diligent and faithful carpenter, carries books in the dusty cab of his work truck and labors in prayer for his family.

My mom, who collected all my newspaper and magazine articles over the years into a little shrine in my childhood home. This encourages me more than you know.

Jon, Bellie, and Bunny, a trio of kids that bring delight to their father! While I wrote they supplied me with a steady stream of encouragement, laughter, joy, and coffee.

And most of all Karalee, who first became my editor, then my friend, and now my wife, and who remains my best friend and my most loyal editor. Somehow you reach out your hands to the poor, love the lost, educate our kids, and smooth my knotted prose. You work with diligence, you love Jesus with a passion, and you laugh enthusiastically at the time to come (Prov. 31:25). Your faith-filled laughter fills our home and frees me to write. To you I promise my life and dedicate this book. I love you!

Notes

Introduction

1. See Herman Bavinck, *Reformed Dogmatics* (Grand Rapids: Baker Academic, 2008), 1:319: "The Reformed theologians were even better positioned to recognize this by their doctrine of common grace. By it they were protected, on the one hand, from the Pelagian error, which taught the sufficiency of natural theology and linked salvation to the sufficiency of natural theology, but could, on the other hand, recognize all the truth, beauty, and goodness that is present also in the pagan world. Science, art, moral, domestic, and societal life, etc., were derived from that common grace and acknowledged and commended with gratitude."

2. I interpret Psalm 36:7–9 as a reference to God's abundant kindness to all his creatures, to both man and beast (v. 6). First, God protects his creatures (v. 7). Second, God provides a rich store of delights for his creatures to enjoy (v. 8). Third, God is the fountain of all the animated life that we find in creation (v. 9a). Fourth, God is the fountain of all light in his creation (v. 9b). This light includes any number of generous gifts and blessings from the Creator, but especially truth, goodness, and beauty. This light in creation is made visible to us because God first illumines us with his glory and presence. Illuminated by God, Christians now perceive and appreciate the light of divine truth, goodness, and beauty that glow in the pages of great books.

Chapter 1: Paper Pulp and Etched Granite

1. Robert Alter, *The Five Books of Moses: A Translation with Commentary* (New York: W. W. Norton, 2008), 425.

2. C. H. Spurgeon, *Metropolitan Tabernacle Pulpit*, vol. 27, *1881* (Pasadena, TX: Pilgrim, 1984 reprint), 124. This quote was modernized and emphasis was added.

Chapter 2: Wide-Eyed into the Son

1. C. K. Barrett, *The Second Epistle to the Corinthians* (New York: Harper & Row, 1973), 121.

2. John Owen, *The Works of John Owen* (Johnstone & Hunter, 1850–1853; repr., Edinburgh: Banner of Truth, 1967), 4:132: "And if any shall suppose or say, that for their part they need no such especial *aid* and *assistance* to enable them to understand the mind of God in the Scripture, which is sufficiently exposed to the common reason of all mankind, I shall only say at present, I am afraid they do not understand those places of Scripture where this aid and assistance is so expressly affirmed to be necessary thereunto."

3. Note how this point was codified by the founders of Harvard College in the *Rules and Precepts Observed at Harvard College* (Sept. 26, 1642): "Let every student be plainly instructed, and earnestly pressed to consider well, the main end of his life and studies is to know God and Jesus Christ which is eternal life (John 17:3) and therefore to lay Christ in the bottom, as the only foundation of all sound knowledge and learning. And seeing the Lord only giveth wisdom, let every one seriously set himself by prayer in secret to seek it of him (Proverbs 2, 3)." Jesus changes how we read science textbooks.

4. John Owen, *Overcoming Sin and Temptation* (Wheaton, IL: Crossway, 2008), 117. This quote has been paraphrased.

5. Martin Luther, "The Gospel for the Festival of the Epiphany, Matthew 2:1–12" in *Sermons II* (ed. Helmut T. Lehmann; trans. John G. Kunstmann and S. P. Hebart; vol. 52 of Luther's Works, American Edition, ed. Jaroslav Pelikan and Helmut T. Lehmann; Philadelphia: Fortress, 1965), 207.

Chapter 3: Reading Is Believing

1. Daniel J. Boorstin, *The Image: A Guide to Pseudo-Events in America* (New York: Vintage, 1992), 13.

2. Neil Postman, *Amusing Ourselves to Death* (New York: Penguin, 1985), 74.

3. David F. Wells, *No Place for Truth, Or, Whatever Happened to Evangelical Theology?* (Grand Rapids: Eerdmans, 1993), 202.

4. Jacques Ellul, *The Humiliation of the Word* (Grand Rapids: Eerdmans, 1985), 1.

5. Carl F. H. Henry, *God, Revelation, and Authority* (Wheaton, IL: Crossway, 1999), 6:50: "The Bible at the very beginning emphasizes that God is not merely an acting God of deed-revelation, but a speaking deity also who shapes language as a medium of intelligible communication with man made in his image. Words are the means of transmitting ideas from person to person: it is not centrally in symbols and visions, but especially in words, that the Old Testament focuses its account of divine-human relationships."

6. Carl R. Trueman, *The Wages of Spin: Critical Writings on Historic and Contemporary Evangelicalism* (Fearn, Ross-shire, Scotland: Mentor, 2007), 44.

7. Ibid.

8. Os Guinness, "The Word in the Age of the Image: The Challenge to Evangelicals," in *The Anglican Evangelical Crisis: A Radical Agenda for a Bible Based Church*, ed. M. Tinker (Fearn, Ross-shire, Scotland: Christian Focus, 1995), 161.

9. John Calvin, *Institutes of the Christian Religion*, ed. John T. McNeill, trans. Ford Lewis Battles (Philadelphia: Westminster, 1960), 1.11.5–7, 12–15.

10. Trueman, *The Wages of Spin*, 48.

11. Geerhardus Vos, *Redemptive History and Biblical Interpretation: The Shorter Writings of Geerhardus Vos* (Phillipsburg, NJ: Presbyterian and Reformed, 1980), 192: "The word remains what it was at the beginning when it fell fresh from the lips of Christ, a signal of the presence of God and a vehicle of approach for the world of the supernatural."

12. Martin Luther, [untitled] in *Lectures on Genesis: Chapters 26–30* (ed. Jaroslav Pelikan, Hilton C. Oswald, and Helmut T. Lehmann; trans. George V. Schick and Paul D. Pahl; vol. 5 of *Luther's Works*, American Edition, ed. Jaroslav Pelikan and Helmut T. Lehmann; St. Louis: Concordia, 1968), 128. Comments on Genesis 27:22.

13. Postman, *Amusing Ourselves to Death*, 73–74.

14. "Peter Hitchens author interview—The Rage against God," Vimeo video, 8:38, http://vimeo.com/10354237. See also Peter Hitchens, *The Rage against God: How Atheism Led Me to Faith* (Grand Rapids, MI: Zondervan, 2010), 101–4.

15. Jacques Ellul, *The Humiliation of the Word* (Grand Rapids: Eerdmans, 1985), 250–51: "John's Gospel insists on sight as long as Jesus is present. His presence on earth is an exceptional time, a unique moment in which it is possible to encounter the fullness of truth by means of sight. The final fulfillment is already taking place. The end of time is present and being *accomplished*. But with Jesus' death and his going to the Father, this period is closed. The Incarnation *has* occurred but it is no longer visible. . . . Fundamentally, John presents Jesus' presence on earth, the Incarnation, as a sort of continual transfiguration. But Jesus' death brings us back to the previous situation. We no longer have any way of seeing Jesus and thus of seeing God. We only hear things said about him. We come back to the word alone and the relationship of faith. . . . Thus as far as I am concerned, everything in Scripture that refers to sight sends us back to this promise concerning sight in the last days, or else to the fact that sight's reconciliation with truth is an eschatological matter."

16. Mark Dever, "Expositional Preaching: A Defense and Charge," lecture given at Southeastern Baptist Theological Seminary, Wake Forest, NC, September 27, 2009). I'm indebted to Dr. Dever for the concepts in this paragraph.

Chapter 4: Reading from across the Canyon

1. Neil Postman, "Learning by Story," *The Atlantic*, no. 264, 1989, 122.

2. Cornelius Plantinga Jr., *Not the Way It's Supposed to Be: A Breviary of Sin* (Grand Rapids: Eerdmans, 1995), 10.

3. D. A. Carson, "The Wrath of God," in *Engaging the Doctrine of God: Contemporary Protestant Perspectives*, ed. B. L. McCormack (Grand Rapids: Baker Academic, 2008), 56.

4. Graham A. Cole, *God the Peacemaker: How Atonement Brings Shalom* (Downers Grove, IL: IVP, 2009), 229. See also Herman Bavinck, *Our Reasonable Faith* (Grand Rapids: Eerdmans, 1956), 22–23: "Science cannot explain this contradiction in man. It reckons only with his greatness and not with his misery, or only with his misery and not with his greatness. It exalts him too high, or it depresses him too far, for science does not know of his Divine origin, nor of his profound fall. But the Scriptures know of both, and they shed their light over man and over mankind; and the contradictions are reconciled, the mists are cleared, and the hidden things are revealed. Man is an enigma whose solution can be found only in God."

5. Daniel L. Migliore, *Faith Seeking Understanding: An Introduction to Christian Theology* (Grand Rapids: Eerdmans, 2004), 139.

6. There are too many references to list. For a sampling see Isaiah 34:4; 51:6; 65:17; 66:22; Matthew 19:28; 24:35; 2 Peter 3:10, 12–13; 1 John 2:17; and Revelation 21:1.

7. Graham Cole, "Do Christians Have a Worldview?," Theology Network, accessed October 28, 2010, http://www.theologynetwork.org/world-religions /getting-stuck-in/do-christians-have-a-worldview.htm.

8. See J. I. Packer, *The Redemption and Restoration of Man in the Thought of Richard Baxter* (Vancouver, BC: Regent College, 2003), 63–69.

9. Grant Horner, *Meaning at the Movies* (Wheaton, IL: Crossway, 2010), 81–82.

10. Herman Bavinck writes: "No doubt among the heathen this wisdom has in many respects become corrupted and falsified; they retain only fragments of truth, not the one, entire, full truth. But even such fragments are profitable and good. The three sisters, logic, physics and ethics, are like unto the three wise men from the east, who came to worship in Jesus the perfect wisdom. The good philosophical thoughts and ethical precepts found scattered through the pagan world receive in Christ their unity and center. They stand for the desire which in Christ finds its satisfaction; they represent the question to which Christ gives the answer; they are the idea of which Christ furnishes the reality. The pagan world, especially in its philosophy, is pedagogy unto Christ," Herman Bavink, "Calvin and Common Grace," in *Calvin and the Reformation: Four Studies*, Geerhardus Vos, ed. (New York: Fleming H. Revell, 1909), 103–4.

11. Gene Edward Veith, "Flex the Brain," *World Magazine*, November 1, 2003, http://www.worldmag.com/articles/8202.

12. As quoted in René Wellek, *A History of Modern Criticism: 1750–1950* (New Haven, CT: Yale University Press, 1955), 130.

13. Frank Kermode, ed., *Selected Prose of T. S. Eliot* (Orlando, FL: Harvest, 1975), 106.

14. Martin Luther, [untitled] in *Sermons on the Gospel of St. John: Chapters 14–16* (ed. Jaroslav Pelikan; trans. Martin H. Bertram; vol. 24 of *Luther's Works*, American Edition, ed. Jaroslav Pelikan and Helmut T. Lehmann, St. Louis: Concordia, 1961), 205. Comments on John 15:2.

15. Peter J. Leithart, "Authors, Authority , and the Humble Reader" in Leland Ryken, ed., *The Christian Imagination: The Practice of Faith in Literature and Writing* (Colorado Springs, CO: Shaw, 2002), 218.

Chapter 5: The Giver's Voice

1. John Calvin, *The Institutes of the Christian Religion*, trans. Henry Beveridge (Edinburgh: T&T Clark, 1863), 2.2.15. Emphasis added.

2. John Calvin, *Commentaries on the Epistles to Timothy, Titus, and Philemon*, trans. William Pringle (Edinburgh: Calvin Translation Society; repr., Grand Rapids, MI: Baker, 2005), 301.

3. John Calvin, *Institutes of the Christian Religion*, ed. John T. McNeill, trans. Ford Lewis Battles (Philadelphia: Westminster Press, 1960), 2.2.16.

4. This is what Brooke Foss Westcott calls "the natural fellowship of men" in *The Victory of the Cross* (New York: Macmillan, 1888), 3–17.

5. Gene C. Fant Jr., *God as Author: A Biblical Approach to Narrative* (Nashville, TN: B&H Academic, 2010), 151–52.

6. Derek Kidner, *Tyndale Old Testament Commentaries: The Proverbs* (Downers Grove, IL: IVP, 1983), 16–17: "The Bible often alludes to the wisdom and wise men of Israel's neighbours, particularly those of Egypt (Acts 7:22; 1 Ki. 4:30; Is. 19:11,12), of Edom and Arabia (Je. 49:7; Ob. 8; Jb. 1:3; 1 Ki. 4:30), of Babylon (Is. 47:10; Dn. 1:4,20, etc.) and of Phoenicia (Ezk. 28:3ff; Zc. 9:2). While the Old Testament scorns the magic and superstition which debased much of this thought (Is. 47:12,13), and the pride which inflated it (Jb. 5:13), it can speak of the gentile sages with a respect it never shows toward their priests and prophets. Solomon outstripped them, but we are expected to be impressed by the fact; and Daniel excelled the wise men of Babylon as one who stood at the head of their own profession (Dn. 5:11,12). Admittedly it was God who gave supernatural insight to these Israelites; but the Old Testament clearly implies that a man can still think validly and talk wisely, within a limited field, without special revelation. This is put beyond doubt by the story of Ahithophel, whose advice continued to be 'as if a man inquired at the oracle of God,' even after he had turned traitor (2 Sa. 16:23; 17:14)."

7. As quoted in George Aaron Barton, *A Critical and Exegetical Commentary on the Book of Ecclesiastes* (New York: Charles Scribner's Sons, 1908), 162.

8. E.g., Duane A. Garrett, *Proverbs, Ecclesiastes, Song of Solomon* (Nashville, TN: B&H, 1993), 264–66.

9. Commentator Rowland E. Murphy is careful to protect the integrity of Proverbs and urges great caution to anyone seeking to find the Egyptian writ-

ings as a source. Yet he concludes, "That the Egyptian source was known, in some form or other, and utilized in this section of Proverbs seems undeniable" (*Proverbs* [Nashville, TN: Thomas Nelson, 1998], 294). See also Derek Kidner's commentary, *Proverbs* (Downers Grove, IL: IVP, 1991), 23–24. Perhaps a copy of *Amenemope* traveled from Egypt and directly influenced Solomon. However, the evidence suggests that the influence was indirect. In his detailed study of this section of Proverbs, John Ruffle suggests that Solomon hired an Egyptian scribe with background education in Amenemope. As Solomon questioned the scribe and learned from him, he took in the teachings of Amenemope, albeit indirectly. See Ruffle's article, "The Teaching of Amenemope and Its Connection with the Book of Proverbs," *Tyndale Bulletin*, vol. 28:1 (Cambridge: Tyndale House, 1977), 29–68. In either case, whether his relationship to *The Teaching of Amenemope* was direct or indirect, Solomon's openness to Egyptian wisdom is equally obvious. With that in mind it is important to make two points. First, as Carl F. H. Henry writes in *God, Revelation, and Authority* (Wheaton, IL: Crossway, 1999), 3:312, "Whatever debt Hebrew writers had to the wisdom literature of other lands, and whatever universal humanistic emphases they share, the Old Testament as an end-product . . . is distinctively Hebrew." And second, as Egyptologist Kenneth A. Kitchen writes, "If Solomon, or anyone else in Jerusalem, had made use of Amenemope (or any other such text from among the Words of the Wise), then they did so critically, using only what seemed to be a suitable expression of what they had approved of, and reset in a Yahwistic mental context" (*Dictionary of Old Testament Wisdom, Poetry, and Writings* [Downers Grove, IL: IVP Academic, 2008], 563).

10. *New Bible Commentary: 21st Century Edition*, 4th ed. (Downers Grove, IL: IVP, 1994), 602. See comments on Proverbs 22:17–24:22.

11. Martin Luther, "Table Talk Recorded by Anthony Lauterback and Jerome Weller 1536–1537" in *Table Talk* (ed. and trans. Theodore G. Tappert; vol. 54 of *Luther's Works*, American Edition, ed. Jaroslav Pelikan and Helmut T. Lehmann; Philadelphia: Fortress, 1967), 210–11: "It is a result of God's providence that the writings of Cato and Aesop have remained in the schools, for both are significant books. Cato contains the most useful sayings and precepts. Aesop contains the most delightful stories and descriptions. Moral teachings, if offered to young people, will contribute much to their edification. In short, next to the Bible, the writings of Cato and Aesop are in my opinion the best."

12. On the non-Christian's ability to perceive moral goodness, see Thomas Goodwin, *The Works of Thomas Goodwin* (Grand Rapids: Reformation Heritage Books, 2006, reprint), 6:231–323. See also John Calvin, *Commentary on the Holy Gospel of Jesus Christ according to John*, trans. William Pringle (Edinburgh: Calvin Translation Society; repr., Grand Rapids, MI: Baker, 2005), 1:173: "I acknowledge, indeed, that some grains of piety were always scattered throughout the whole world, and there can be no doubt that—if we may be allowed the expression—God

Notes

sowed, by the hand of philosophers and profane writers, the excellent sentiments which are to be found in their writings. But, as that seed was degenerated from the very root, and as the corn which could spring from it, though not good or natural, was choked by a huge mass of errors. . . ."

13. Leland Ryken, Jim Wilhoit, and Tremper Longman III, eds., *Dictionary of Biblical Imagery* (Downers Grove, IL: InterVarsity Press, 2000), 82.

14. Leland Ryken, ed. *The Christian Imagination: The Practice of Faith in Literature and Writing* (Colorado Springs, CO: Shaw, 2002), 151.

15. Richard J. Mouw, *He Shines in All That's Fair: Culture and Common Grace* (Grand Rapids, MI: Eerdmans, 2001), 37.

16. For more on the historical details of this paragraph see F. F. Bruce, *The Book of Acts* (Grand Rapids, MI: Eerdmans, 1988), 338–39.

17. See David G. Peterson, *The Acts of the Apostles* (Grand Rapids, MI: Eerdmans, 2009), 500. On what basis does the apostle Paul identify genuine spiritual truth in the writings of ignorant pagan poets who are suppressing the truth? I admit this is a tricky question. In my own research I have been helped by nineteenth-century Dutch theologian Herman Bavinck and his outstanding work *Reformed Dogmatics*, ed. John Bolt, trans. John Vriend, 4 vols. (Grand Rapids, MI: Baker Academic: 2003–2008). Especially helpful are his arguments on pages 1:301–22, 1:507–10, 2:53–78, 3:238–40, and 4:179–80. If that looks intimidating, these same points are condensed in Bavinck's *Reformed Dogmatics: Abridged in One Volume*, John Bolt ed. (Grand Rapids, MI: Baker Academic, 2011), on pages 68–73, 113–14, 155–64, 403, and 553.

18. Bavinck, *Reformed Dogmatics*, 1:319–320. Bavinck makes a similar point when he shows how the idea of substitutionary atonement is reflected in non-Christian literature. He writes, "The idea of substitution is deeply grounded in human nature. Among all peoples it has been embodied in priesthood and sacrifices and expressed in various ways in poetry and mythology" (3:403). He cites the literary examples of Codrus, Curtius, Cratinus, Zaleucus, Damon, and Phintias. Similarly, tragedies teach that "all human greatness walks past abysses of guilt, and satisfaction occurs only when what is noble and great, which for some reason has gone astray, perishes in death" (3:403). He cites the examples of Orestes, Oedipus, Antigone, Romeo and Juliet, Max and Thekla, and Iphigenia. All these characters are "illustrations of the substitutionary suffering of Christ" (3:402). But they are nothing more than illustrations. Nonetheless, by reading classic literature in light of the cross, Bavinck models how Christians today can also read and appreciate the illustrations.

19. Basil, "Address to Young Men on the Right Use of Greek Literature," in Frederick Morgan Padelford, *Essays on the Study and Use of Poetry by Plutarch and Basil the Great* (New York: Henry Holt, 1902), 104, 120.

20. Augustine, *On Christian Doctrine*, in *The Nicene and Post-Nicene Fathers*, first series, ed. Philip Schaff (Peabody, MA: Hendrickson Publishers, 1994), 2:554.

21. Ibid.

22. David Lyle Jeffrey, *People of the Book: Christian Identity and Literary Culture* (Grand Rapids: Eerdmans, 1996), 87: "What Augustine advocates is not a syncretism but a discriminating borrowing according to fixed and ordinate principles laid down in Scripture itself."

23. Calvin, *Institutes*, Battles, 3.20.34.

24. Ibid.

25. Calvin uses Plato as an example of the spiritual blindness of even the keenest pagan minds. In the *Institutes* he writes of the sinful impulse in the heart to "substitute monstrous fictions for the one living and true God—a disease not confined to obtuse and vulgar minds, but affecting the noblest, and those who, in other respects, are singularly acute" (*Institutes*, Beveridge, 1.5.11,). Plato is here included as one who is in other regards "astute." Calvin did not overlook the theological blindness of Plato.

26. Calvin's language is careful regarding human depravity. On one side, Calvin believes that non-Christian authors can perceive spiritual truth. But due to sin, any spiritual truth perceived cannot be assembled into a cohesive system of thought. For the author they are fleeting thoughts. But for the Christian reader these are insights into the gracious working of the Giver that we can, and should, appreciate (see *Institutes*, Battles, 2.2.18).

27. John Piper, "The Ethics of Ayn Rand: Appreciation and Critique," June 1, 1979, rev. October 9, 2007, http://www.desiringgod.org/resource-library/articles /the-ethics-of-ayn-rand.

28. John Piper says, "To this day, I find her [Ayn Rand] writings paradoxically attractive. I am a Christian Hedonist. This is partly why her work is alluring to me. She had her own brand of hedonism. It was not traditional hedonism that says whatever gives you pleasure is right. Hers was far more complex than that. It seems so close and yet so far to what I find in the Bible," from "The Ethics of Ayn Rand."

29. Mouw, *He Shines in All That's Fair*, 93.

30. Cornelius Plantinga, *Engaging God's World: A Christian Vision of Faith, Learning, and Living* (Grand Rapids, MI: Eerdmans, 2002), x.

31. John M. Frame, "Unregenerate Knowledge of God," The Works of John Frame and Vern Poythress, http://www.frame-poythress.org/frame _articles/2005Unregenerate.htm.

32. Basil, "Address to Young Men on the Right Use of Greek Literature," in Frederick Morgan Padelford, *Essays on the Study and Use of Poetry by Plutarch and Basil the Great* (New York: Henry Holt, 1902), 104.

Chapter 6: The God Who Slays Dragons

1. Herman Bavinck, *Our Reasonable Faith* (Grand Rapids, MI: Eerdmans, 1956), 18: "Man's thinking and knowing, although bound to his brain, are nevertheless

in their essence quite entirely a spiritual activity, far transcending the things he sees with his eye and handles with his hand."

2. G. K. Beale, *The Book of Revelation: The New International Greek Testament Commentary* (Grand Rapids, MI: Eerdmans, 1999), 351.

3. D. A. Carson, *Scandalous: The Cross and Resurrection of Jesus* (Wheaton, IL: Crossway, 2010), 84.

4. D. Brent Sandy, *Plowshares and Pruning Hooks: Rethinking the Language of Biblical Prophecy and Apocalyptic* (Downers Grove, IL: IVP, 2002), 127–28.

5. Kevin J. Vanhoozer, *The Drama of Doctrine: A Canonical-Linguistic Approach to Christian Theology* (Louisville, KY: WJK, 2005), 281.

6. C. S. Lewis, "Bluspels and Flalansferes: A Semantic Nightmare" in Walter Hooper, *C. S. Lewis: A Complete Guide to His Life and Works* (San Francisco: Harper, 2005), 570. Emphasis added.

7. Greg Beale, "The Key to Understanding Symbolism," sermon given at Desert Springs Church, Albuquerque, NM, May 19, 2007. See also Beale, *Revelation*, 177: "The symbols in Revelation have both a hardening effect on the unbelieving and a shock effect on genuine saints caught up in the church's compromising complacency."

Chapter 7: Read with Resolve

1. John Calvin, *Commentary on the Holy Gospel of Jesus Christ according to John*, trans. William Pringle (Edinburgh: Calvin Translation Society; repr., Grand Rapids, MI: Baker, 2005), 2:73.

2. John Calvin, *Commentaries on the Epistles of Paul to the Galatians and Philippians*, trans. William Pringle (Edinburgh: Calvin Translation Society; repr., Grand Rapids, MI: Baker, 2003), 264.

3. C. S. Lewis writes in the introduction to Athanasius, *On the Incarnation: The Treatise De Incarnatione Verbi Dei* (Crestwood, NY: St. Vladimir's Seminary, 1996), 8: "For my own part I tend to find the doctrinal books often more helpful in devotion than the devotional books, and I rather suspect that the same experience may await many others. I believe that many who find that 'nothing happens' when they sit down, or kneel down, to a book of devotion, would find that the heart sings unbidden while they are working their way through a tough bit of theology with a pipe in their teeth and a pencil in their hand."

4. Elyse Fitzpatrick, "Publications for Christian Women," *The Journal of Biblical Counseling* (Spring 2003): 60–69.

5. Ibid.

6. Marilynne Robinson, *Gilead* (New York: Picador, 2004), 57.

7. Gary A. Stringer, ed., *The Variorum Edition of the Poetry of John Donne*, vol. 7, *Part 1: The Holy Sonnets* (Bloomington, IN: Indiana University, 2005), 25. This excerpt was lightly modernized.

8. Gene Edward Veith, *Reading between the Lines: A Christian Guide to Literature* (Wheaton, IL: Crossway, 1990), 162.

9. C. S. Lewis, *An Experiment in Criticism* (Cambridge: Cambridge University, 1961), 68.

10. Alan Jacobs, *The Pleasures of Reading in an Age of Distraction* (Cambridge: Oxford University Press, 2011), 17.

11. James W. Sire, *How to Read Slowly: Reading for Comprehension* (Wheaton, IL: Shaw, 1989), 157.

12. Robert Frost, *The Robert Frost Reader: Poetry and Prose*, ed. Edward Connery Lathem and Lawrance Thompson (New York: Henry Holt, 2002), 440.

13. *The Works of Shakespeare* (London: Isaac, Tuckey, and Co., 1836), viii, *Google* books, http://bit.ly/litoo1.

14. Sire, *How to Read Slowly*, 158.

15. Harold Bloom, *How to Read and Why* (New York: Scribner, 2000), 29.

16. C. S. Lewis, *The Screwtape Letters* (New York: HarperCollins, 2001), 64.

Chapter 8: How to Read a Book

1. Mortimer Adler, *How to Read a Book* (New York: Toushstone, 1972), 75.

2. Francis Bacon, *The Essays: Or, Counsels Civil and Moral of Francis Bacon* (D. C. Heath & Co., 1908), 158.

3. John Piper, "Quantitative Hopelessness and the Immeasurable Moment," sermon given at Bethlehem Baptist Church, Minneapolis, MN, July 12, 1981, http://www.desiringgod.org/resource-library/sermons/quantitative-hopelessness-and-the-immeasurable-moment.

Chapter 9: Literature Is Life

1. Horatius Bonar, *Follow the Lamb; Or, Counsels to Converts* (London: James Nisbet & Co., 1874), 45.

2. J. I. Packer in *The Gospel in Dostoyevsky: Selections from His Works* (Ulster Park, NY: Plough, 2004), vii: "His plots and characters pinpoint the sublimity, perversity, meanness, and misery of fallen human adulthood in an archetypal way matched only by Aeschylus and Shakespeare, while his dramatic vision of God's amazing grace and of the agonies, Christ's and ours, that accompany salvation, has a range and depth that only Dante and Bunyan come anywhere near. Dostoyevsky's immediate frame of reference is Eastern Orthodoxy and the cultural turmoil of nineteenth-century Russia, but his constant theme is the nightmare quality of unredeemed existence and the heartbreaking glory of the incarnation, whereby all human hurts came to find their place in the living and dying of Christ the risen Redeemer."

3. Leland Ryken, *Windows to the World: Literature in Christian Perspective* (Eugene, OR: Wipf and Stock, 2000), 176.

4. A point well made by the ancient Greek philosopher Aristotle when contrasting fictional poetry with history. Aristotle writes: "It is not the poet's function to relate actual events, but the kinds of things that might occur and are possible in terms of probability or necessity. The difference between the historian and the poet is not that between using verse or prose. . . . No, the difference is this: that the one relates actual events, the other the kinds of things that might occur. Consequently, poetry is more philosophical and more elevated than history, since poetry relates more of the universal, while history relates particulars. 'Universal' means the kinds of things which it suits a certain kind of person to say or do, in terms of probability or necessity: poetry aims for this" (Aristotle, *Poetics*, trans. Stephen Halliwell [Cambridge, MA: Harvard University Press, 2005], 59, 61).

5. Flannery O'Connor, *Mystery and Manners* (New York: Farrar, Straus, & Giroux, 1969), 123.

6. Ibid., 163.

7. Leland Ryken, *Realms of Gold: The Classics in Christian Perspective* (Eugene, OR: Wipf and Stock, 1991), 5.

8. Flannery O'Connor, *Collected Works* (New York: Penguin Books, 1988), 863: "There is something in us as story-tellers, and as listeners to stories, that demands the redemptive act, that demands that what falls at least be offered the chance of restoration. The reader of today looks for this motion, and rightly so, but he has forgotten the cost of it. His sense of evil is deluded or lacking altogether, and so he has forgotten the *price* of restoration. He has forgotten the cost of truth, even in fiction."

9. Chris Stamper and Gene Edward Veith, "Get Real: Master of Reality Fiction, Acclaimed Author Larry Woiwode Has Found Christ, But Can He Find an Audience?," *World Magazine*, July 4, 1998.

10. Flannery O'Connor, *Mystery and Manners* (New York: Farrar, Straus, & Giroux, 1969), 167.

11. O'Connor, *Collected Works*, 805.

12. Grant Horner, *Meaning at the Movies: Becoming a Discerning Viewer* (Wheaton, IL: Crossway, 2010), 82–83.

13. P. D. James, interview by Ken Myers, *Mars Hill Audio Journal*, journal 100.

14. Ryken's *Realms of Gold: The Classics in Christian Perspective* is available in book format (Eugene, OR: Wipf and Stock, 1991) and online as an audio book from Mars Hill Audio (marshillaudio.org). I've read the book twice and listened to it at least three times. I learn something new every time.

15. Alan Jacobs, *The Narnian: The Life and Imagination of C. S. Lewis* (New York: HarperCollins, 2005), 349: "Almost everything that Lewis really cared about and that he deeply believed in, almost everything that he thought was vital for us to know, no matter how scholarly, no matter how intellectual, found its way somehow into the Narnia books—to a shocking degree, actually. You wouldn't

think that he would be able to get all that stuff into a series of what are, after all, relatively brief books for children, and yet he did." To more fully appreciate the depth of the Narnia Chronicles, consider reading a couple of companion volumes like Douglas Wilson's *What I Learned in Narnia* (Moscow, ID: Canon Press, 2010) or Michael Ward's *Planet Narnia: The Seven Heavens in the Imagination of C. S. Lewis* (Oxford: Oxford University Press, 2008), which was later simplified into *The Narnia Code: C. S. Lewis and the Secret of the Seven Heavens* (Grand Rapids, MI: Tyndale House, 2010).

16. Leland Ryken, *Windows to the World*, 34.

Chapter 10: Too Busy to Read

1. Robert Lee, *Religion and Leisure in America: A Study in Four Dimensions* (Nashville, TN: Abingdon, 1964), 37.

2. C. S. Lewis, *The Weight of Glory* (San Francisco: HarperOne, 2001), 60.

3. Alan Bissett, "Who Stole Our Reading Time?" *Books Blog, The Guardian*, February, 2010, http://www.guardian.co.uk/books/booksblog/2010/feb/02/who-stole-reading-time.

4. National Endowment for the Arts, *To Read or Not to Read: A Question of National Consequence*, no. 47, November 2007, http://www.nea.gov/news/news07/TRNR.html.

Chapter 11: Driven to Distraction

1. David L. Ulin, "The Lost Art of reading," *Los Angeles Times*, August 09, 2009, http://articles.latimes.com/2009/aug/09/entertainment/ca-reading9.

2. Nicholas Carr, "Is Google Making Us Stupid? What the Internet Is Doing to Our Brains," *The Atlantic Magazine* (July/August 2008), http://www.theatlantic.com/magazine/archive/2008/07/is-google-making-us-stupid/6868/. Carr later authored a book on the topic, *The Shallows: What the Internet Is Doing to Our Brains* (New York: W. W. Norton & Company, 2010).

3. Susan Jacoby, *The Age of American Unreason* (New York: Vintage, 2009), 263.

4. See Maryanne Wolf, *Proust and the Squid: The Story and Science of the Reading Brain* (New York: HarperCollins, 2007), 51–78.

5. Reginald Hackforth, trans., *Plato's Phaedrus* (Cambridge: Cambridge University, 1952), 157.

6. Clive Thompson, "Your Outboard Brain Knows All," *Wired Magazine*, September 25, 2007, http://www.wired.com/techbiz/people/magazine/15-10/st_thompson.

7. Carr, "Is Google Making Us Stupid?"

8. Douglas Groothuis, "Why Truth Matters Most: An Apologetic for Truth-Seeking in Postmodern Times," *Journal of the Evangelical Theological Society* (September 2004): 453.

9. Kevin Kelly, *Smithsonian*, August 2010, http://www.smithsonianmag.com /specialsections/40th-anniversary/Reading-in-a-Whole-New-Way.html.

10. Thomas Brooks, *Precious Remedies against Satan's Devices* in *The Works of Thomas Brooks*, 6 vols. (Edinburgh: Banner of Truth, 1980), 1:8.

Chapter 12: Marginalia

1. John Piper, "The Ministry of the Word," sermon given at Bethlehem Baptist Church, Minneapolis, MN, November 25, 1984, http://www.desiringgod.org /resource-library/sermons/the-ministry-of-the-word.

2. H. J. Jackson, *Marginalia: Readers Writing in Books* (New Haven, CT: Yale University Press, 2002), 88.

3. John Piper, "The Pastor as Theologian: Life and Ministry of Jonathan Edwards," lecture given at 1988 Bethlehem Pastors Conference, Minneapolis, MN, April 15, 1988, http://www.desiringgod.org/resource-library/biographies /the-pastor-as-theologian.

Chapter 13: Reading Together

1. C. H. Spurgeon, *Metropolitan Tabernacle Pulpit,* vol. 58, *1912* (Pasadena, TX: Pilgrim, 1979 reprint), 429.

2. Marilynne Robinson, *The Death of Adam: Essays on Modern Thought* (Boston: Houghton Mifflin, 1998), 117.

3. Rick Ritchie, "The Well-Read Christian: Why Bible-Lovers Should Be Bibliophiles," *Modern Reformation* (July/August 1994): 18–23.

4. Ibid.

Chapter 14: Raising Readers

1. The Henry J. Kaiser Family Foundation, *Generation M2: Media in the Lives of 8- to 18-Year-Olds*, http://www.kff.org/entmedia/mh012010pkg.cfm.

2. Tamar Lewin, "If Your Kids Are Awake, They're Probably Online," NYTimes .com, January 20, 2010, http://www.nytimes.com/2010/01/20/education/20wired .html.

3. Thomas Spence, "How to Raise Boys Who Read," WSJ.com, September 24, 2010, http://online.wsj.com/article/SB10001424052748704271804575405511702112290.html.

4. Douglas Wilson, "Opening Every Lawful Door," *Blog & Mablog*, October 10, 2009 (page discontinued).

Chapter 15: Happily Ever After

1. Duane A. Garrett, *Proverbs, Ecclesiastes, Song of Songs* (Nashville, TN: B&H, 2001), 344: "The contrast is not between the study of canonical versus nonca-

nonical wisdom but between failure to appreciate wisdom on the one hand and excessive zeal for study on the other."

2. C. S. Lewis, *An Experiment in Criticism* (Cambridge: Cambridge University, 1961), 2.

3. C. S. Lewis, "Introduction," in St. Athanasius, *On the Incarnation: The Treatise De Incarnatione Verbi Dei* (Crestwood, NY: St. Vladimir's Seminary, 1996), 5.

4. Ibid., 9.

5. C. S. Lewis, *Christian Reflections* (Grand Rapids: Eerdmans, 1967), 10. Emphasis added.

6. John Newton, *Wise Counsel: John Newton's Letters to John Ryland Jr.*, ed. Grant Gordon (Edinburgh: Banner of Truth, 2009), 127.

7. C. H. Spurgeon, *Metropolitan Tabernacle Pulpit*, vol. 49, *1903* (Pasadena, TX: Pilgrim, 1977), 43.

8. John Piper, *God's Passion for His Glory: Living the Vision of Jonathan Edwards* (Wheaton, IL: Crossway, 1998), 29: "If a book is easy and fits nicely into all your language conventions and thought forms, then you probably will not grow much from reading it. It may be entertaining, but not enlarging to your understanding. It's the hard books that count. Raking is easy, but all you get is leaves; digging is hard, but you might find diamonds."